BECOMING AN EMPOWERED SURVIVOR

BECOMING AN EMPOWERED SURVIVOR

YOU, TOO, CAN HEAL FROM TRAUMA AND ABUSE

ELIZABETH M. JONES

SCORPIO RISING PUBLISHING

Becoming an Empowered Survivor: You, Too, Can Heal from Trauma and Abuse

Copyright 2024, © Elizabeth M. Jones

All rights reserved. No part of this publication may be reproduced or transmitted in any form or by any means, mechanical or electronic, including photocopying and recording, or by any information storage and retrieval system, without permission in writing from the author (except by a reviewer, who may quote brief passages and/or show brief video clips in a review).

Disclaimer: This book reflects the author's present recollections of experiences over time. Some names have been changed, details have been limited, or details have been modified to protect privacy. Other events were omitted, compressed, or fabricated, and dialogue has been recreated using journal entries, text messages, and memory. The content is not intended to provide medical advice. If you are suffering as a result of trauma and abuse, please seek appropriate medical help.

ISBN: 979-8-9904305-0-1 (paperback)

Edited by Jocelyn Carbonara
Cover and interior design by George Stevens, G Sharp Design, LLC
Published by Scorpio Rising Publishing, LLC | Dallas, TX

Publisher's Cataloging-in-Publication Data
Names: Jones, Elizabeth M., 1970-
Title: Becoming an empowered survivor : you, too, can heal from trauma and abuse / Elizabeth M. Jones.
Description: Dallas, TX : Scorpio Rising Publishing, 2024. | Summary: As a survivor of trauma and abuse who has taken the hero's journey, the author believes that to HEAL is to hope, evolve, and love—as action words. She details her journey, told as a tale of courage and resilience to inspire other survivors to break free of their past.
Identifiers: LCCN 2024912751 | ISBN 9798990430501 (pbk.)
Subjects: LCSH: Elizabeth M Jones, 1970- , — Biography. | Abused women. | Psychic trauma. | Healing. | BISAC: SELF-HELP / Abuse. | SELF-HELP / Motivational & Inspirational. | FAMILY & RELATIONSHIPS / Abuse / General.
Classification: LCC HV6625.J66 2024 | DDC 362.8292 J--dc23
LC record available at https://lccn.loc.gov/2024912751

*Dedicated in loving memory to
Amelia Jimnell Jones Garner, my "Aunt Cheeto," whose
suffering in this life ended the day I committed to writing this
book. Her lifelong trials inspire me as I seek to help others find
and walk their healing pathway. She never had the opportunity to heal, but in death, I hope she is at peace with her
God. The day she died, my "why" for writing this book and for
whom became clear. This book is dedicated, with honor,
to her life.*

*This book is also dedicated to
every trauma and abuse survivor in this
world who needs to HEAL.*

TABLE OF CONTENTS

Foreword ix

Preface xvii

Introduction 1
Trauma, Unhealthy Survivorship, and Healing

Part 1   THE NEED TO HEAL 9

    Chapter 1 11
    Surviving Life

    Chapter 2 31
    Uncovering Truths

    Chapter 3 51
    Acknowledging Walls

Part 2   HOPE 79

    Chapter 4 83
    Losing Optimism

    Chapter 5 91
    Reigniting Resolve

Part 3   EVOLVE 103

    Chapter 6 107
    Exploring Healing Tools

    Chapter 7 135
    Engaging in Self-Discovery

Chapter 8 175
Learning to Mirror

Chapter 9 181
Reframing the Hardest Parts

Part 4 LOVE 193

Chapter 10 203
Fostering Self-Love

Chapter 11 207
Addressing Hurtful Relationships

Chapter 12 231
Embracing Healthy Relationships

Part 5 TOOLS TO HEAL 239

Conclusion 257
Helping Us Heal

Epilogue 263

Acknowledgments 271

About the Author 277

Join the Empowered Survivors Community 279

Bring Beth to Your Support Team 281

Bring Beth to Your Stage 283

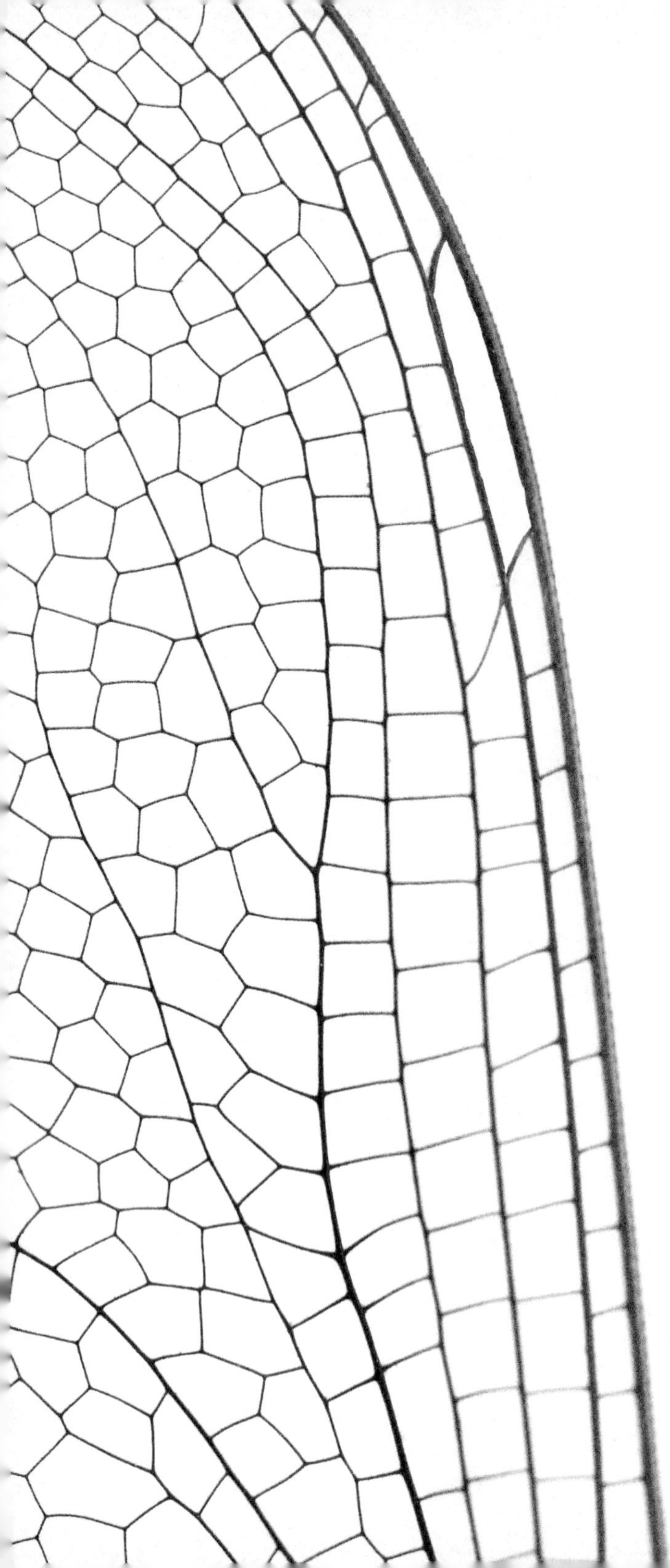

FOREWORD

AS HUMAN BEINGS, we succeed as a species by evolving. Part of our evolutionary conditioning involves reacting to traumatic events so that we can survive. This is because most of our traumas happen so quickly that we don't have time to access the thinking part of our brains; it's quicker for us to react than to think about how to respond. These immediately available reactions are commonly known as *fight or flight*, although we may also show *freeze and fawn* reactions. Only when our brains emerge from this survival state can we process these events and recover from their effects on our lives.

Post-trauma is often when survivors begin to experience a range of associated, intense emotions that may prevent them from leading whole, healthy lives. For example, often, a survivor will blame themself for not doing more to avoid the trauma. Blame frequently leads to shame, wherein a survivor wears the misplaced responsibility of those who caused the harm. Blame and shame can cause this survivor to feel hopeless and helpless. And because the perpetrator of most traumatic events is someone who the survivor expected to love and protect them, this survivor is often left feeling unsafe, unloved, and unlovable. Consequently, they may struggle to recover and trust themself and others.

Trauma may also cause a reaction of avoiding people, places, or events that remind the survivor of what happened to them. Avoidance, however, can leave unprocessed trauma in the body, sometimes stored in the darkest recesses of the mind. When this happens, a person can be flooded with adrenaline, dissociation, and hypervigilance, with no readily available explanation for their reactions.

Dissociation is our brain's way of surviving pain—causing a survivor to feel out of their body, unreal, or checked out. Dissociation can make it hard to be present in everyday activities. A survivor might find themself spacing out, losing track of time, or spending hours immersed in gaming, binge-watching TV, or other addictive behaviors.

In contrast, hypervigilance occurs when our survival system is on high alert, often evidenced by an over-awareness of noise and threats. Our mind sends false alarms, tricking us into feeling danger when, in fact, we are safe. This can confuse a survivor because they can't separate actual versus imagined threats. Therefore, the mind and body work in a feedback loop, preventing this survivor from thriving. Hypervigilance can also cause this survivor to retreat from the world in an attempt to find safety.

A survivor can heal once they're aware that they need to. The healing journey may begin when a survivor knows that they feel differently than before, even when they aren't sure why. They might be curious why they feel uncomfortable in their skin or are attracted to certain people. Becoming aware of how trauma is harming self-worth, relationships, and the ability to function is paramount to the success of the healing process. The challenge is being brave enough to do the work to process the trauma because the work itself is not easy.

This work includes going to the emotional places the survivor has avoided. These places can make survivors vulnerable, as they may relive the horror of the abuse or trauma. This is when deep levels of shame can be revealed as someone recounts what they may have done—or not done—while in survival mode. Specific treatment modalities, such as eye movement desensitization reprocessing (EMDR) and brainspotting, allow the survivor to release the trauma and associated emotions from their body without too much speaking.

Though processing trauma can be painful, avoiding it can cause more harm, as it most likely will come out in negative ways. Someone's brain might try to process what happened through physical or emotional flashbacks, which can be more painful than the original events. Their survival system, which keeps them alive, might be on high alert—hypervigilant—until their mind and body learn that they're safe.

The risk of living in survival mode is three-fold, at least.

First, survivors might not have a baseline for a normal, healthy relationship and may repeat the same patterns they have been in previously. They might unknowingly be attracted to abusive people and find themselves in other traumatic situations. Sometimes, the original abuse is not as intense or painful as the current abuse.

Second, unprocessed trauma and the associated emotions wear down the mind and body as survivors suffer under the weight of survivorship. This can manifest in a variety of ways, including self-isolation, a weakened immune system, inflammation, anxiety, and depression. A survivor might also feel like they are abnormal, when in fact they are normal. This is when a survivor might have immense shame and low self-worth.

And perhaps most detrimental is the likelihood that survivors will harm otherwise healthy relationships with people who they need as part of their support system. Survivors often struggle to trust others in everyday events and might fear allowing others in will cause more harm. The consequence can be a fearful attachment style, wherein they might both crave and fear emotional intimacy. This internal struggle leads to pushing away those who try to get too close to the survivor. And at its worst, the abused may become the abuser.

As I know her, Beth is a survivor—and now a thriver. She has done the work to overcome the constraining grip that her survivorship—resulting from unprocessed trauma and her associated emotions—had on her life.

When I first met Beth, she protected herself by living behind a wall. While her wall kept her safe from feeling pain because it kept others out, worse for her was that she was trapped there, alone. From the beginning of our work together, Beth struck me as independent, intelligent, and strong, yet she often questioned her self-worth and whether she was lovable. She also questioned her repressed memories and soon learned that she didn't repress memories. Instead, she dissociated during her traumatic events, causing her not to record in her memory all the information about what was happening to her.

Though Beth had been harmed, she wasn't one to harm others. Instead, she developed an amazing sense of empathy and generosity. Though Beth had suffered intense attachment wounds and trauma, she never lost her ability to love and trust. Instead of pushing others away, she allowed people into her life to the best of her ability, always seeing the best in them. Beth could intuit and selflessly offer what other people needed, yet she could not ask others to meet her needs.

Beth's ability to hope and persevere helped her overcome the challenges of processing her trauma. Though she was in a foreign land, facing her past and new traumas, including her divorce, she never gave up. Her perseverance and grit got her through the dark nights into the next day's light.

I've often gotten chills along Beth's journey. I've witnessed ethereal moments as she learned to have self-compassion, quiet her inner critic, and see her worth. I've witnessed moments of inspiration as she was able to objectively distance herself from and forgive some of the abuse, finding grace for and acceptance of her perpetrators. And I've seen moments when she was in action, and I knew she was meant to be a healer. Today, Beth has completed the hero's journey, conquered her trauma, and arrived on the other side as someone who can help others heal.

As Beth's healing progressed and her wall fell, I could see how authentic, compassionate, and empathetic she was. I've walked with her through her healing journey, which has resulted in her ability to love and be loved.

Not too long ago, she sent me a passage that someone wrote to her. When I read it, I saw the embodiment of who she is and why her message about healing—to hope, evolve, and love—is essential to engage in healthy and loving human-to-human relationships—not only for survivors but ultimately for each of us.

> *Love is awareness. It is being present in every moment and cherishing the beauty and connection between two souls. It is the ability to truly see and understand each other, embracing strengths and vulnerabilities. Love is a constant state of mindfulness, where you are attuned to the needs and desires of the other person and are willing to support and nurture their growth. It is a deep appreciation for the small and grand gestures alike, knowing that each act of love can create a ripple effect of happiness and warmth. Love is fully engaging in life's journey together, celebrating the joys, and navigating the challenges hand-in-hand. It is the ultimate expression of empathy, compassion, and understanding, creating a bond that transcends time and space. Love is the fuel that ignites the soul, bringing light, warmth, and meaning to our existence.*

This book was written for anyone wanting to heal, trust, and love. All survivors are fighters, but that is just the beginning of your journey. Beth is a model for healing, and her strategies are powerful. But above all, her belief in herself is the most powerful. Within these pages is the inspiration to help you overcome the effects of your unprocessed trauma and associated emotions and heal.

Monica Borschel, PhD

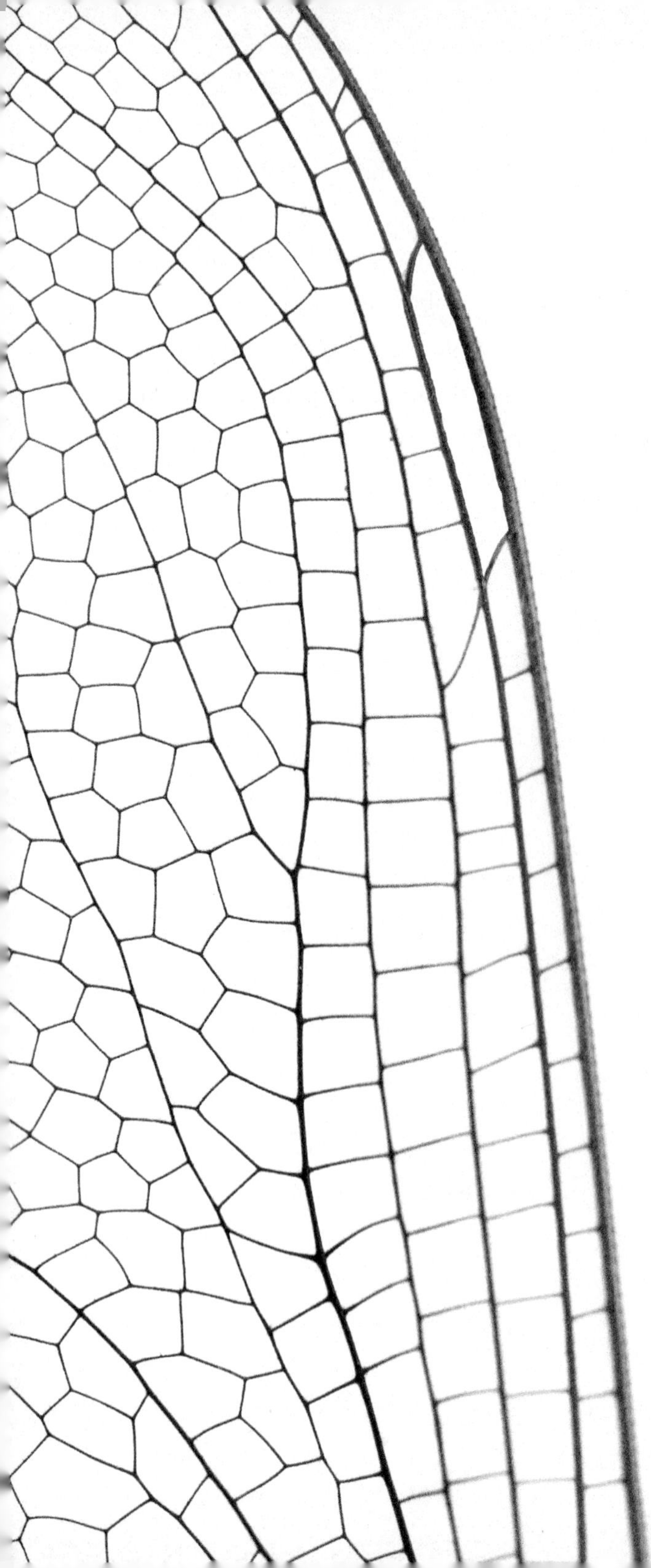

PREFACE

AUTHOR'S NOTE

I'M A LIVING testament to the freedom, joy, and love a survivor of trauma and abuse can find by choosing to *heal* and journey with focus and intention. For some time now, I have known my life path was leading me to help others heal by holding a safe space where I could teach and mentor them. Since my journey began, the steps of my path have unfolded naturally before me, forming my evolution to this place. I feel I'm now equipped with enough of my own experiences and lessons that I can help others.

Getting my story out to those who need to hear it—our community of Empowered Survivors—began about one year into my healing journey. Around this time, I began to realize the power of this story, my story. This understanding came through self-discovery to clarify my purpose and what I'm meant to do with my power. My life's purpose has included suffering as a victim, surviving, and healing—ultimately so that I can teach others about the power of healing and the joy and love available when anyone chooses to heal. I learned that my power to share this message comes from the unique combination of who I am, what I've survived, how I've survived, the dichotomy of my personal and professional life, and the beauty of my healing journey.

I've shared my story with many people who have intersected with the ordinary course of my life, but I know a more extensive community out there needs my help. The Universe wants me to assist my community—abuse and trauma survivors like me who need to heal. I know my work and purpose are more significant than what I already do. I must reach a broader community with my hope, evolution, and love message. So, I wrote this book to do just that.

For a couple of months, before I decided to write, I'd been discussing my views on forgiveness with my trauma therapist. Her curiosity about my thinking on this concept started our conversations. That sparked my interest—another step on my journey—in seeing what other authors said about forgiveness. So, I began researching what was written and found a few things that bothered me. I saw why there's so much confusion about forgiveness, what it is, and how we can get it.

There are many, many books on the "steps" to forgiveness. To me, *steps* suggest a linear process required to arrive at forgiveness. In my experience, this isn't accurate and is not how my healing has worked.

I've read books by authors who say you must forgive to heal. This is also not true in my experience. Instead, for me, letting go—a result of my healing process—isn't always the same as forgiveness. I've let go of the negative emotions about those who have hurt me, feelings that would otherwise constrain my heart and keep me from the joy I find through love.

Letting go has come through discovering why people may have acted to harm me. As I understood the reasons for my behavior, I began to reflect on my understanding of myself toward those who hurt me. That gave me grace for and acceptance of them, and I simply let go. But I have not forgiven them because what they did to me is unforgivable.

I've read material from other authors who say the inverse, that you must heal to forgive. While this is closer to what I believe, I do not think it is a must/then or cause/effect principle. This notion suggests to me that an objective of healing is to eventually be able to say, "I forgive you for whatever horrible thing you did to me." How can we say these words about an action done to us that is, again, unforgivable?

My path to help others heal began long before my recent journey; it started the moment I was born. I'm a double Scorpio, where both my sun and ascendant signs are Scorpio. My life seems to be mostly about bringing light to darkness and exposing secrets held in the shadows, which is explained by the Scorpio and Scorpio Rising aspects of my natal chart.

Indeed, I spent more than twenty years of my career bringing light to corporate darkness, including revealing the secrets of alleged wrongdoers or fraudsters. As a forensic accountant investigating white-collar crime, my job was to sift through mountains of information to find the specific evidence that revealed the hidden scheme by which a fraud was perpetrated. In that way, I brought light to the secret of their wrongdoing. Think of me as Sherlock Holmes meets the Enron scandal.

But that life is now behind me. Today, I know my calling is to help others bring light to the darkness of their suffering, as I have done for myself.

More recently, I read David Brooks's book, *The Second Mountain: The Quest for A Moral Life*. I feel like his words were written just for me. He discussed how *first mountain* people focus on the individual—serving self-interest or the ego. These people may concentrate on climbing the corporate ladder and fulfilling self by accumulating titles, salaries, and material possessions. I lived on my first mountain for fifty years.

Second mountain people are in service to others. They deeply commit to community, vocation, family (my interpretation of his reference to marriage), and/or spirituality (my interpretation of his reference to religion). Many people go through a transformative event between the first and second mountains, followed by a time in their lives when they are in the valley between their two mountains.

I have been in my valley since June 2020, when I experienced my most transformative event, the awakening of my unconscious state of being. I thought hypnotherapy would be a benign process, but my session radically changed the trajectory of my life forever. And now, I believe I've been in the valley for long enough. The Universe is ready for me, urging me to climb my second mountain. This book is a significant step forward.

A lot of people in this world are suffering, some of them living encumbered by *unhealthy survivorship*. That's my phrase for all the harmful coping mechanisms we as survivors use to continue living after enduring trauma and abuse. Outward signs of the trauma impacting people in unhealthy ways—like addiction, depression, and suicide—are more obvious. But I know firsthand that many survivors cope inwardly—in ways no one can see that still cause harm.

I've read these people's stories of survival and recovery. They share their stories for the good of others in a growing societal movement to bring light into this world. They have found their way to me, using me as a mentor and sharing their story in reciprocation as I have begun to tell my story publicly. This is me with my story.

Many of us have done the work to heal. Many others—perhaps you—have not yet but are now ready to stop their suffering caused by merely surviving. They want to thrive by finding joy and love. If this is you and you're ready to heal, I hope my story will inspire you to find and walk your healing pathway.

If you're already walking your pathway, I hope my story will encourage you to keep going, no matter how you feel now or during the most challenging parts of what lies ahead of you.

And I hope you will see, through my story, that the hard parts get easier. As I've healed, my unhealthy survivorship has been replaced, mostly, by healthier ways of living and engaging in relationships. As I've healed, I have found joy and love. So, I know that you, too, can heal from your trauma and abuse.

If you're not quite there in deciding to heal, I hope my story will inspire you to go over the precipice and commit to yourself. Committing to healing may be the first act of genuine love you experience. This is self-love—which is crucial for us as survivors—but self-love can be tough. In my experience, loving yourself enough to shed unhealthy survivorship and work toward thriving is the greatest gift you can offer yourself.

This book is meant to tell you my story about my healing journey, including the work I have done and still do to mitigate and manage my unhealthy survivorship. It's also meant to be a reference book that can be part of your healing toolkit. However, this book is not a how-to or step-by-step guide to the healing process. While I've found my path and now help others as a healing mentor, I'm not a trained mental health professional. And for me to suggest I know how to heal you would be arrogant and disrespectful of the real and very specific nature of what you've survived and how it has affected you. No two of us are exactly alike in what we have experienced, and so, too, the healing journey is unique to each of us. I only hope my story inspires you to find your unique healing techniques, your unique use of tools, and your unique way of thinking. But more importantly, I hope my story inspires you to *heal*.

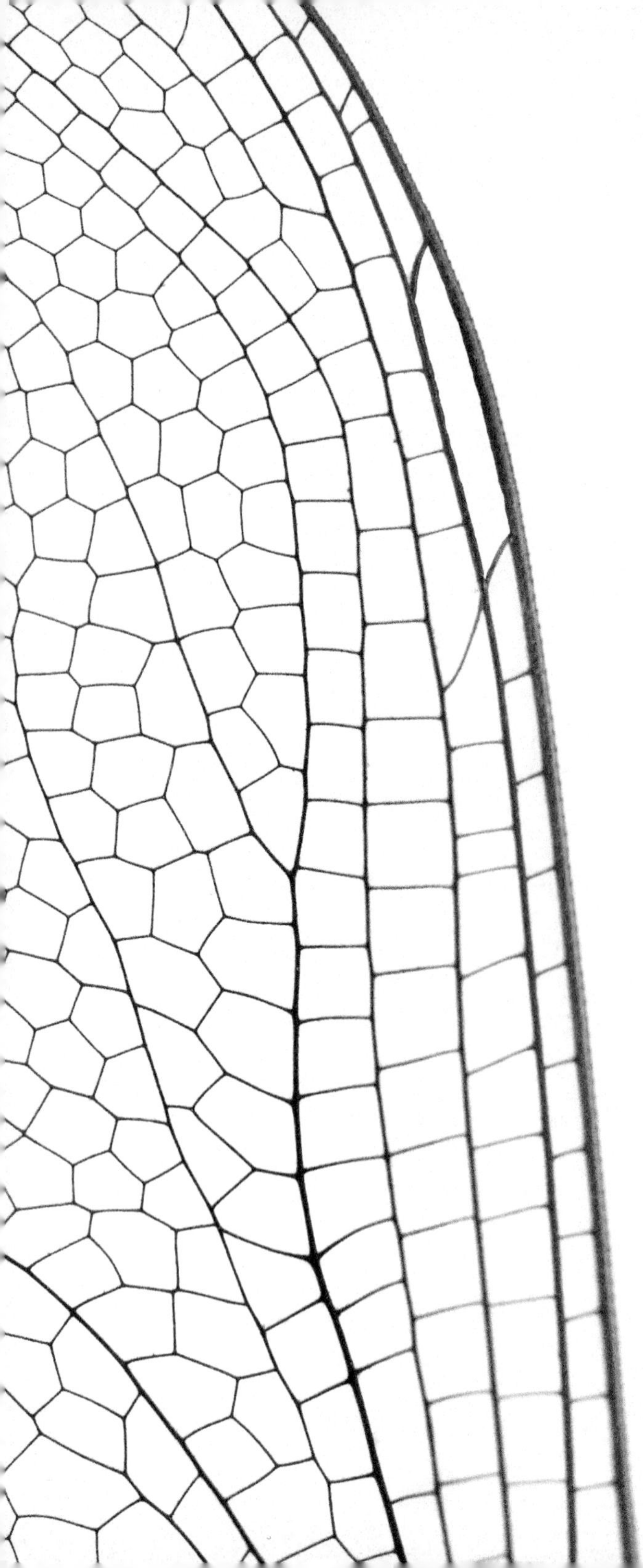

INTRODUCTION

TRAUMA, UNHEALTHY SURVIVORSHIP, AND HEALING

> Trauma knows no demographic boundaries. It doesn't care who you are or where you come from. Neither age, gender, race, religion, nor socioeconomic status can protect you from trauma and survivorship. The only way to protect yourself from unhealthy survivorship—and end your suffering—is to heal.

I AM BOTH a victim and a survivor of trauma. I've read about trauma and trauma response for my healing purposes. And I've heard people talk about their trauma and abuse. Through these inputs, I've developed my understanding and beliefs about trauma, unhealthy survivorship, and healing, which I'll be describing in this book in my own layman's language.

Trauma

Trauma is a human condition that disempowers a survivor. We all have and will suffer trauma in one way or another during our lives. Some of us, like me, suffer sustained trauma over time.

Sustained trauma can result from significant events—what I think of as macro traumas—the effects of which remain with us for a very long time, perhaps forever. We see this in the lingering physical and emotional toll of being sexually abused. Or the lingering physical and emotional toll of a chronic, life-threatening illness. Or the forever void in our very existence created with the loss of a child, the loss of a parent when we were a child or even the tragic loss of a beloved pet.

Sustained trauma can also come from the constant layering of what I think of as micro traumas. These include our daily encounters with anyone whose actions or words cause us to hurt, even in the slightest way. For example, this may include a spouse displaying contempt through their facial expressions or not showing up to support us on the worst day of our lives. Or a parent's inability to nurture their child emotionally after a difficult day at school or when their best friend moves away. Or a workplace environment where an encounter with a colleague includes sexual harassment.

Sometimes, perhaps often, macro trauma is filled with micro traumas. Divorce is a macro trauma. The events and effects surrounding a divorce—the daily hurtful encounters caused by, or with, our significant other before, during, and after the Divorce Day—are all micro traumas.

I don't believe the severity of trauma and abuse can be ranked by degrees. Instead, its impact is measured in the receiving person's response, based on who they are and what they have experienced. Some people react negatively to an event, while others may perceive it as minor or a micro trauma. Yet other people will move through what some may consider to be a heinous, traumatic event with strength and resiliency. Perhaps this is just a reflection of who they are. Or maybe they are sufficiently healed to react this way.

Unhealthy Survivorship

As survivors, our lives are reflected in how we respond to trauma and abuse. If we react negatively, we probably rely on unhealthy coping mechanisms that don't serve us. If we respond more positively, we're probably healthier and using better coping skills and tools.

Unhealthy survivorship develops on the flipside of the same coin where we survive our trauma and abuse. While trauma differs for everyone, living encumbered by *unhealthy survivorship* is something many of us have in common.

Unhealthy survivorship—which I will talk about a lot in this book—again is my phrase for the negative ways we, as survivors, cope with events that harmed us. The impact of our unhealthy survivorship on how we live causes us increased and prolonged suffering.

We can't do anything about what happened to us in the past, but we can overcome our unhealthy ways. We can overcome substance abuse. We can overcome suicidal ideation. We can overcome our own emotional and physical abuse of others. We can overcome our fight, flight or freeze responses. We can quiet our hateful inner critic. But more importantly, we can find love and engage in healthy, supportive relationships, including with ourselves. We just need to heal.

Healing

Suffering is also a human condition that occurs if we don't heal. There are two reasons, at least, for why we should heal. First, we should heal for ourselves because none of us needs to suffer encumbered by unhealthy survivorship. By not healing, we never find peace, and we never thrive. I'm not a fan of absolutes; "never say never," as the saying goes, and I've learned this lesson at least a dozen times. In this instance, however, I think the absolutes of *never finding peace* and *never thriving* are almost always correct descriptors of our lives if we don't heal.

The second primary reason to heal is to be positively influential—rather than harmful—to people we hold relationships with. I've seen firsthand in my family the broad, generational destruction that one person's abuse can inflict on so many, regardless of whether they suffered the abuse directly. My grandfather was an unhealed survivor who abused some of us directly. Indirectly, he placed tremendous suffering on those closest to him across four generations. Nearly every family in his lineage has suffered somehow, and I can see how it all ties back to the person he was.

I've also witnessed firsthand the destruction that unhealed trauma has had on others who are not my blood relatives. With my now ex-husband, for example, my marriage was, in effect, a casualty of my healing process. He, too, is a survivor of his trauma, but I believe he chose not to heal in a way that may have allowed us to remain together. His survival tactics for his trauma—primarily, being a busyholic in chronic chaos—inflicted a lot of pain on me. And my choice to heal caused the end of our marriage. We both suffered.

More recently, I chose to exit a relationship with someone whose self-destructive behavior all but destroyed our relationship. I loved him deeply but chose to leave because living with him was too painful for me. It was too painful for me to watch what he did to himself to cope with being an unhealed survivor and too painful for me to be the recipient of the abuse that too often came with his behavior. We both suffered.

Some people say by not healing, we allow our abusers to win. I don't believe that is true. I think abusers lose regardless because they likely were abused in some way themselves and never had their own opportunity to heal. By not healing, they also miss the experience of joy and love that comes from healthy relationships.

Others say healing is the best form of revenge. I don't think healing ever involves getting even, which is implicit in the idea of revenge. Getting even, revenge, and hatred are different shades of the same concept. Harboring such feelings only perpetuates our own suffering while also entrapping the other person in our own negative projections.

Not healing perpetuates the entangled and often extensive bondage that unhealthy survivorship places on us and our family unit. It's hard to be a positive influence on our children and grandchildren. It's hard to be a positive influence on our nieces and nephews. It's hard to positively impact those we work with, especially when we serve in a leadership role with greater responsibility for others. It's hard to have authentic relationships with our friends. And it's hard to be truly present in our spiritual houses and the communities where we live and serve.

Most of my relationships have become richer through healing. This is because I now know that to *receive* genuine love, I must be able to *accept* love and *give* it back. Healing has enabled me to engage with love in each of these ways. I'm more able to contribute positively to my relationships, as I'm filled with and surrounded by love.

Men and Women, We're All the Same

People who need to heal aren't bound by age, gender, race, sexual orientation, or socioeconomic status because trauma knows none of these as boundaries. Of these traits, the one I believe to be most problematic to navigating healing is gender. Not feeling safe to admit trauma, unhealthy survivorship, and the need to heal comes up almost every time I talk with men who are survivors. They feel society's judgment, which generally teaches us that men should be strong and resilient, no matter what, and therefore, they don't have anything to heal from. If they do experience trauma, they're somehow expected to just *get over it*. Or when they need help, they think they shouldn't admit it, or else they may appear weak. They believe any attempt to get help should be done in secret. These are all ridiculous judgments, in my opinion.

Males can be hurt in all the same ways females can, and to say otherwise is unfair. The emotional toll of macro and sustained micro traumas can be just as impactful, regardless of gender, and we all can experience the same unhealthy survival methods. As human beings, we're all the same. Therefore, we're all *emotional beings*.

We're also the same in that we can **heal**. We can all have **hope**. We can all **evolve**. And we can all know **love**.

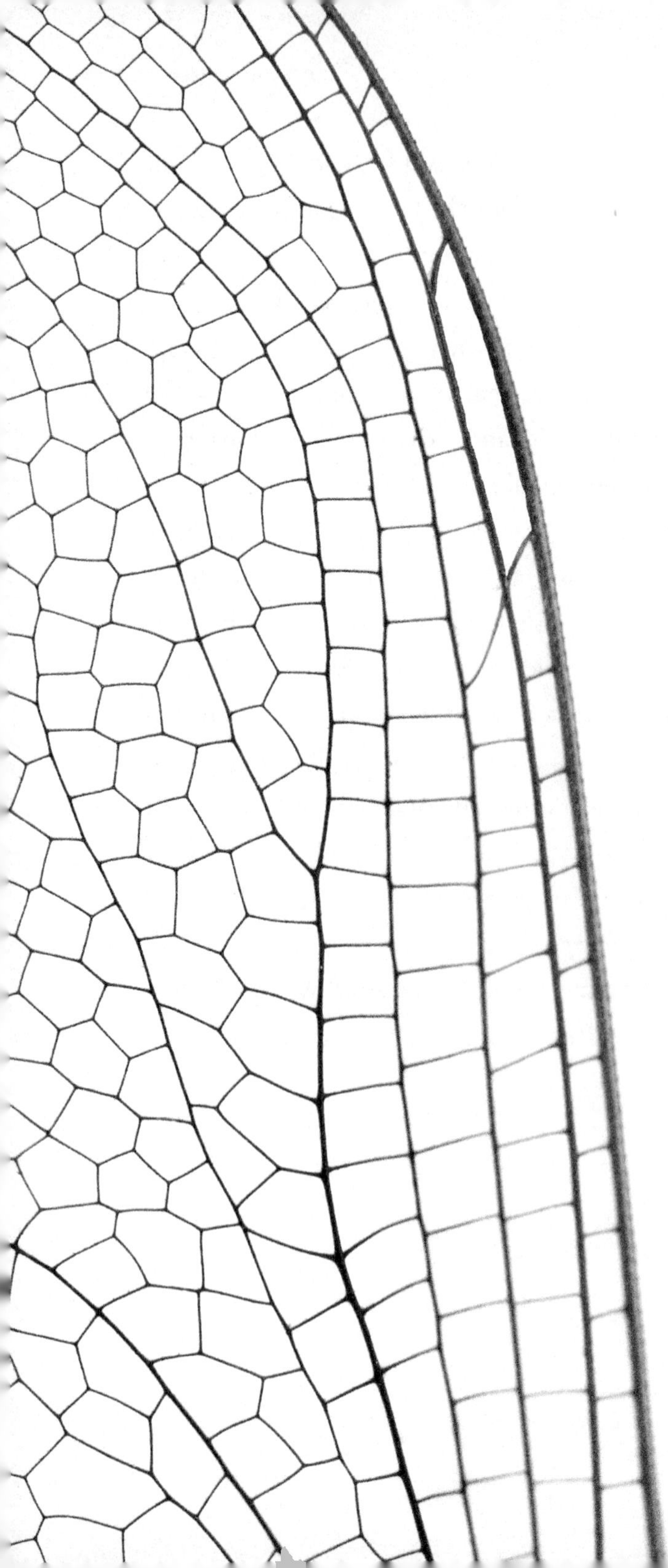

PART I

THE NEED TO HEAL

While the intention of this book is to share my story about healing, I must lay the foundation for why I needed to heal and give you a glimpse into my life as a survivor. I may look like you in some ways. Perhaps in many ways.

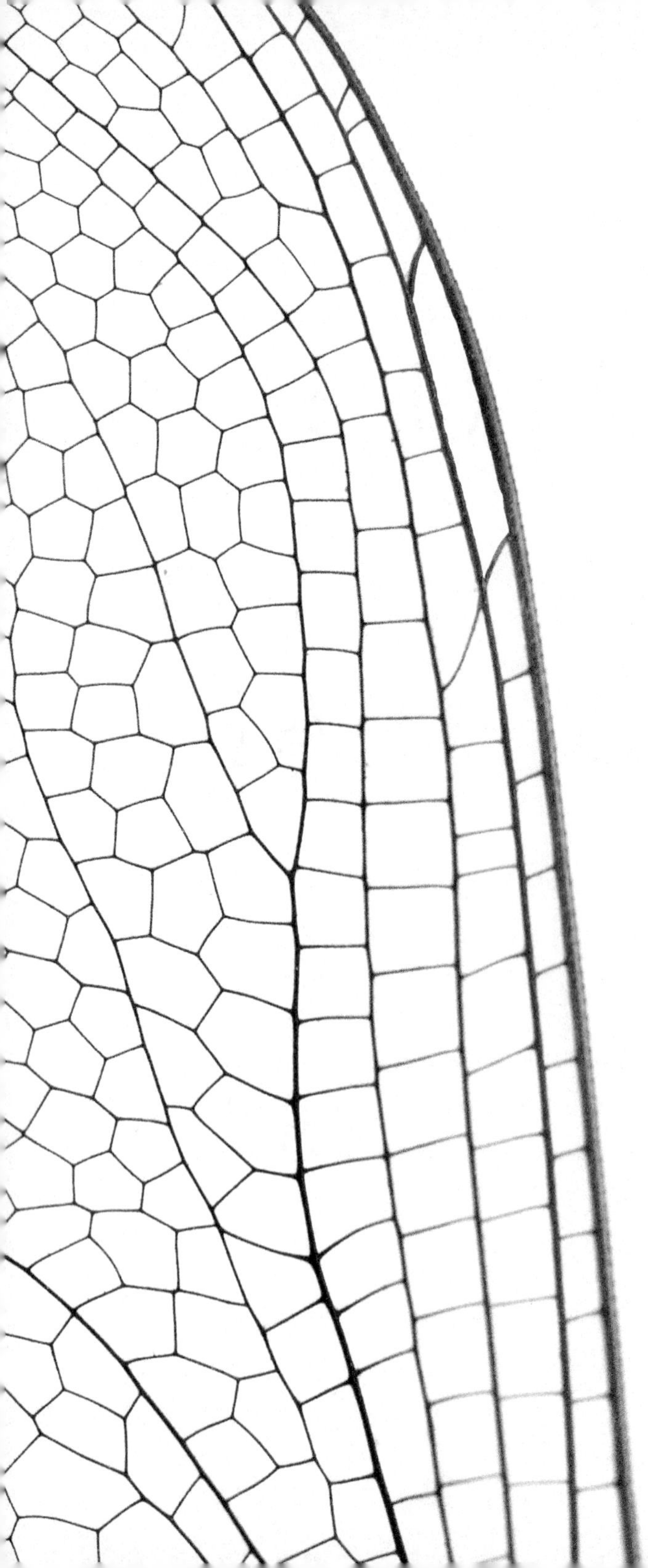

CHAPTER 1

SURVIVING LIFE

I WAS ONCE told not to write about my life chronologically, and this book is not my memoir. Some historical account of certain pivotal events in my life seems appropriate, however, to lay out the traumas I've survived, both macro and micro. Chronology is also appropriate to describe the progression of the mounting pressure to heal that I experienced before the day my life changed forever. So please indulge me as I take you through a bit of my life's history. Not everything, but you'll get the idea. Then, I'll embellish and tell you more as I reveal my healing journey.

These accounts are fact-based and emotionless. It is fitting to be written this way at the beginning of my story, where I'm going to describe for you how I have transformed and evolved from being emotionless in response to my trauma and abuse to knowing and dealing with my emotions as I healed. And please understand that this is what I did so well for so long, professionally: telling the facts, and only the facts, as if none of this has anything to do with me.

My Macro and Micro Traumas

When I was five years old, just a few months before my sixth birthday in 1976, I experienced my first sexual abuse and became a survivor. It was summertime, and we were visiting my Aunt Cheeto and my cousins—her daughters, Jeannine, Jeannette, and Deanne. My grandparents on my dad's side were there, too. At the time, I don't know whether my parents knew we would be leaving the country and moving from the US to Dubai, United Arab Emirates. Perhaps this was one of the last family gatherings before we departed.

My cousins and I often played hide-and-seek with my grandfather as young kids. That's when it happened. He and I were hiding in the bathroom—me sitting on his lap, my tiny legs straddling one of his legs. As we sat there, waiting to be sought, the fingers of his enormous hand moved over my legs, between my legs, and in me. With his other hand, he stroked himself. It ended abruptly when we were found in the game.

For years after we moved away from the US, I experienced a lot of change growing up, living in five different cities in different parts of the world and experiencing different cultures. I completed kindergarten through second grade in Dubai.

Then, we lived in Singapore for grades three and four and in two different cities in Indonesia for grades five through twelve. I completed middle school in Balikpapan, on the island of Borneo, and high school in Jakarta, on the island of Java, where I graduated.

I experienced culture shock when I moved from Jakarta, a predominantly Muslim city and one of the world's largest and most densely populated, to Commerce, a small college town deep in East Texas. That's where I attended East Texas State University. (Today, it's known as Texas A&M-Commerce.) I was a foreigner in that place, proclaiming to be "from Indonesia." My friends used to call me "Indonesia Jones."

My oddities, which some of my college friends still see today, can only be explained by me being that foreigner. I'm a citizen of the world, not one country, with many of my foreign experiences lingering today. Get my sister and me together, and our English—neither American nor Texan—will be laced with Arabic and Indonesian words. My spelling is atrocious and wrong to Americans because I tend to "favour" the use of "ou" rather than just "o" in words like "favor." (Neither is incorrect, but my way aligns with British English more than American English.)

I grew up with two parents who were also survivors. The manifestation of their survivorship impacted my life in profound ways, the same as it does for everyone who lives with an unhealed survivor. My dad was Jekyll and Hyde. Literally, when I saw his reflection in a mirror, the face I saw wasn't the same face as when I looked at him directly. This was a strange phenomenon I couldn't explain, but an excellent metaphor for the person he once was. He is my dad, but at times he was just another person suffering under the weight of his own unhealthy survivorship.

My mom believed in the generalizations about the firstborn child, perpetuating the order and perfection of that mythical child on me, which allowed me to flourish as the "perfect" child. The mythical me also came with my mom's perception that I was independent and could care for myself (which became a reality as I grew and matured). Even as a kid, this belief allowed her caregiving nature to divert to the two other people who demonstrated more of a need for her attention than I could: my dad and my sister, Natalie.

The dysfunction in our home got bad starting in 1980 as I turned ten years old. That's when we moved from Singapore to Balikpapan for my dad's job. His role at that time brought the epitome of what salespeople did back in the day (and not so far back) to entertain and win business—starting with a lot of alcohol consumption. That's when Jekyll became Hyde. My parents would fight. Sometimes violently. Natalie and I would sequester in one of our rooms, almost always physically safe, until it was over. It would be years before my mother could share with me what my parents endured when they fought.

If you know the real meaning of "Jekyll and Hyde," you'll know there is no good Jekyll and bad Hyde. Instead, Hyde is a mask over Jekyll, concealing the reality of who he is. For years, until I graduated from high school and left home, Hyde hid my dad from who he was—hid my dad from me. The man

I would come to know as I got older and reaped the rewards of my focused and intentional healing was no Hyde at all. He's my dad, who loves me. And he's a cycle breaker, never perpetuating the sexual abuse of my grandfather on me.

I was date-raped, bullied, and betrayed during my sophomore year of high school when I was fifteen. I had a crush on the boy who became my abuser—a good-looking, popular upperclassman. He was a peacock, consuming what people fed him about his looks and popularity. At the time, I had barely begun to blossom as a woman and still had remnants of the awkward, gangly teenager I was outgrowing. Still, he invited me to be his date at a school dance. Today, I believe asking me to be his date was to fulfill a bet that he could get me to have sex with him.

I don't recall anything about the dance itself. Though somewhat vague, my memory picks up in the backseat of a taxi. I was successful in fighting him off from penetrating me. But unsuccessful as he straddled me, forcing me into oral sex. I was exhausted from the fight and deflated as I saw the taxi driver mocking me with his eyes through the rearview mirror.

The following Monday at school, everyone was whispering and laughing at me. I had not satisfied him—giving him what he wanted—so he told people I "gave head like I was sucking a popsicle." Then, people teased me almost daily for the rest of the school year, which was at least three months. "Popsicle" was pounded into my head repeatedly, relentlessly. Most of my friends even took part in the teasing and bullying.

Others were silent and said nothing to defend me—betraying me, though not intentionally. For some of us, this was just the cruel reality of being in high school.

At some point, BJ, my initials for the name I go by, Beth Jones, also applied to "blow job" and became the replacement for "Popsicle." I have this weird thing with my neck where my blood becomes like ink in a pen when someone "writes" on it with something pointed, like their finger. Whatever is written there stays, in clear detail, for several minutes until my blood fades away. Schoolmates would pin me down and write *BJ* on my neck. That continued through my senior year, though the boy who started it all was long gone, and I don't think most people who were engaging in the trick by then even knew what its genesis had been. But I remembered. *Every. Single. Time.*

The entire series of events I experienced in high school contributed to losing trust in people in general. Yes, what the boy and taxi driver did to me was part of that, but what the rest of my schoolmates did is what seriously impacted me in this way.

Early in my sophomore year of college, I met and started dating my husband, Tristan, just before my nineteenth birthday in 1989. We were set up on a blind date and became inseparable almost immediately. We married in 1992 when I was twenty-one. As I've shared, he, too, is a survivor, so our life together was riddled with manifestations of our unhealthy survivorship. For me, that meant ongoing micro traumas that layered into something much more problematic, becoming its own macro trauma.

A couple of years after Tristan and I married, we bought what we thought would be our forever home in a small town called Myrtle Springs, Texas. We lived there for ten years, working happily together to put down our roots. But for some reason that I'll never really understand, perhaps the burgeoning of his ego and a mid-life crisis, we started to do things like buy second homes. We had no business doing that; we didn't have that kind of money. But he wanted to, and I didn't have a voice to say "no." This began a twenty-year cycle of chasing ever-elusive happiness that we never found. All we found was chaos.

In 2007, we moved to our first, second home in Combine, Texas. We justified this second home because it was closer to Dallas than our mini-ranch in Myrtle Springs and a little closer to work. Before then, we commuted sixty miles daily each way.

We hired a caretaker couple to live in the house in Myrtle Springs and take care of our land and animals, since most of them—the livestock—remained there when we moved to Combine. The caretakers smoked marijuana, and being high was all they seemed to care about. Their caretaker work was almost nonexistent, and we constantly reacted to some crises they caused or couldn't handle. For example, when our cows got out and roamed around the roads and other people's property for hours until we got off work and rounded them up. The caretakers were so high they had no idea the cows were even out. I think the county sheriff called and told us about the problem. We were probably on his speed-dial list because that wasn't our first or last call from his department.

The worst part of living in Combine was the hatred we experienced from the townsfolk, generally, and by the town's pillars—in particular, Christians and the city council—over our servals. Servals are exotic cats, the smallest of the Africans. We raised them for twenty-five years and moved them to Combine with us. Our life was controlled by all the animals we cared for, but our servals exerted next-level control over us. We could rarely go away for more than a couple of days' respite because getting someone else to feed them their raw diet daily was almost impossible. Though not aggressive, they are expressive when hungry and don't like strangers. Most people feared the unknown.

We were always in a mode of protecting the cats because, over the years, the laws in Texas changed significantly to control possession by irresponsible owners. These changes have increased public awareness of exotic animals living next door. Because servals were classified by the state of Texas as "dangerous wild animals," along with lions, tigers, bears, and elephants, people reacted with visceral fear when they learned the cats lived nearby. But the fear was completely unfounded. My miniature schnauzer had a more severe bite than our servals.

The hatred in Combine began immediately as we properly petitioned the city council to approve our servals living on our property, which was within the city limits. By law, even though they were legal in our county and we were given an indication that they would be allowed, we needed this permission from the city. In the process of waiting for this formal approval, we suffered a mob mentality from residents who were fueled by the "dangerous wild animal" label. People trespassed on our property to take pictures—evidence of the cats' existence. A petition against us was signed one Sunday morning as churchgoers—the Christians—entered their church, and a city council meeting was orchestrated in a certain way to result in a decision against us, immediately forcing us out of the city. Never in my life had I experienced as much hatred directed at me as during those months.

The city council decision meant we literally had to move out of Combine overnight. Our next stop was twenty-plus acres in Kaufman, Texas. But the land wasn't ready for us and all the animals we would eventually accumulate there. So, building the ranch life—and all the chaos that came with that process—began again for the second time.

When we took on the property in Kaufman, we had mortgages on the properties in Myrtle Springs and Combine. We couldn't afford all three (who can?!), so we found someone to rent the property in Combine. At first, we had a personal relationship with the renter. But for some reason, I don't remember why, our relationship ended—wholly and abruptly. We evicted the renter.

I'm not sure which example best illustrates the disastrous condition of the house and property after he left. Was it the fifteen dogs and the spare tires placed around the yard to cover up massive holes his dogs had dug under the fence, coupled with the foul stench of dog shit everywhere? Or the anarchy signs painted blood red on the walls in one of the bedrooms? Or the bullet holes in the walls of the metal building in the backyard? Or...Tristan's reaction? Rescuing him from his reaction was a great example of me stepping into my normal operating mode of extreme problem-solving, wherein I perpetually disregarded my emotions or needs.

We bought the property in Kaufman less than six months after purchasing the property in Combine. It had taken all our savings to buy the place in Combine, and we were already living on a tight budget, paycheck-to-paycheck, to make it all work. Being run out of Combine, forced to find the down payment and closing costs to buy the property in Kaufman, then moving (again) and cleaning up other people's messes meant we were hemorrhaging cash. The situation was untenable, and something had to give.

By this time, most of our possessions had been moved to Kaufman. So, selling our forever home in Myrtle Springs was the best option to relieve the pressure. Although it was a painful decision for both of us, it was ultimately the right one.

Though Tristan never got over it. (You'll understand more about that later.) Instead of selling Myrtle Springs, Tristan wanted to file for bankruptcy. He almost *demanded* bankruptcy in a fit of anger, which was how he reacted to the thought of selling his beloved Myrtle Springs.

"This is stupid! Just stupid! File f'ing bankruptcy, and to hell with all of it!" he screamed at me, over and over again one day, in a fit of rage.

After a few months, I worked us through the pain—without filing for bankruptcy. I wouldn't let us. I had credentialed myself professionally through my licensure as a certified public accountant (CPA), and I knew the licensing board in Texas frowned on bankruptcy. Our financial livelihood would have been in jeopardy had I followed Tristan's wishes, and the ensuing additional problems would still be with me today.

This was one of the only times I exerted my will in our relationship, and it probably marked the turning point for me making most of the financial decisions for the rest of our time together. My pushback to his bankruptcy demand was very rare, indeed, but I knew the consequences for us—for me—had we gone that route.

By this time, I was becoming the financial provider anyhow. Tristan had worked various full-time jobs for the first twelve years we were married. Then, as we were dealing with the transition from Myrtle Springs to Kaufman, a series of events that happened to him—including being knocked unconscious and mugged, literally left for dead, and a couple of run-ins with the law over driving under the influence—pushed him out of the workforce. He tried, unsuccessfully, to build his own businesses. So, his identity became tied to caretaking our properties and the animals. I acquiesced, and he assumed the role for the next eighteen years.

Today, I believe that providing for and protecting my financial livelihood is a gift from the Universe. I've always been blessed with the financial means to meet my needs. God has always seen fit to keep a roof over my head and put food on my table despite other hardships. In the past, a Higher Power provided for many, many of our wants despite years of us not being good stewards over much of the money given to us.

In 2014, my employer transferred me from Texas to the town of Conifer, west of Denver, Colorado. The move took weeks and required two semitrucks and about fifteen trips, with Tristan and me hauling a thirty-five-foot flatbed trailer loaded full of farm equipment and supplies. Plus, we had to make special trips to move our animals—the serval cats, too—which were illegal for citizens to own in Colorado. We basically smuggled them from Texas to Colorado and then hid them in an enclosure that wasn't visible unless you were invited to, or trespassed on, our property.

Our place was technically in the foothills by Rocky Mountain standards, but to Texans, it was fully in the mountains at 8,600 feet of elevation. Much maintenance and care were required to deal with the frequent and sometimes catastrophic weather events. Neither our servals nor our goats belonged in that cold and snowy environment. Servals are native to sub-Saharan desert grasslands; ours had only previously experienced winter in Texas. And our goats were easy prey for the mountain lions.

Neither did I belong in that environment.

"If we're moving to Colorado, I'm not moving 'flat to flat,'" Tristan had threatened. He was referring to the east side of Denver, which is flat, like the eastern part of Texas from which we were moving. "We're moving to the mountains!"

Again, I thought, *Whatever might make him happy and keep the peace.* I had no voice.

Over the years, we endured and recovered from three house floods—one in Kaufman and two in Conifer. Twice, we attempted planned remodel work—in Myrtle Springs and Kaufman—but sued the contractors for shoddy and incomplete work. Marijuana plants sprouted the following spring from the site where one contractor's work trailer had sat for months. Our goats were even offended. They wouldn't touch the plants, even though goats are infamous for eating anything and everything.

Another time, a building flooded and caused us to be without water at our house in Kaufman for several days because a heifer had put her head through the side of a building, right where the water filtration system for our house was. The house in Combine had a fifty-pound, live-bee honeycomb in the joists between the first and second stories, and the septic system was completely infiltrated with massive tree roots. Of course, we didn't know any of this when we bought the property. We closed on the purchase during the coldest part of winter in Texas, which kept visible and olfactory signs of both problems at bay, and the inspector "missed" both.

Just after moving to Conifer, we had massive hail damage to all our vehicles and tractors, and our well pump there was struck by lightning. We futilely tried to replace the pump, but were forced to drill a brand-new well. For weeks, while we waited our turn for the drilling company, we hauled water from thirty miles away to keep our house functioning.

Add to all this the fifteen or sixteen (I lost count at some point) surgeries Tristan underwent during our time together. Each resulted from an accident or wear and tear on his body because of his and our lifestyle. None of his injury stories are sensational or traumatic. The circumstances are all relatively mundane. But the constant revolving door of injury, surgery, recovery, and repeat wore on me, physically and emotionally. I was playing nurse to someone who increasingly—and understandably—grew frustrated with his inability to perform in the way he wanted to physically. When he wasn't recovering, his body just wouldn't do what he wanted it to, and he became almost fragile. That state of being wore him down emotionally and only compounded how he responded to me when things didn't suit him. I lived in fear of injuring him—and of his reaction if I did—when we worked together on our properties almost daily, repairing whatever needed it.

I moved to Hong Kong in 2016 because of another job transfer. Although we were meant to be in Hong Kong together full-time, dealing with the problems and crises in the US was Tristan's role while I was working. We hired a caretaker, again, for the house and animals in Conifer. But over our years of hiring caretakers, we never hired anyone who knew what they were doing. This time, we hired a former model and bartender with no experience in caretaking or with Colorado mountain winters. So the constant problems, and sometimes full-on crisis, continued in Conifer. If Tristan spent eight months in Hong Kong during my almost six years there, that's a generous estimate.

Conifer would be the last place for me and that chaotic life. When I left, I walked away quietly with a coffee table and twelve bankers' boxes containing the few possessions I wanted—mostly childhood and college memorabilia and a few Christmas ornaments. I learned later that the box of Christmas ornaments was full of items that reflected good parts of my life that I'm now happy to remember. Felt gingerbread men and Raggedy Ann and Raggedy Andy made of yarn from my first Christmas tree, handmade by my mom's mother so I could play with them. And ornaments representing every country I had ever lived in, the Komodo Dragon mascot of my high school in Jakarta, and my Texas heritage. The coffee table had once belonged to my mom's mother, "Elizabeth." I am her namesake.

Tristan left in July 2020, five weeks after I'd had my hypnotherapy session, during the lowest and darkest point of my life. He was going to Thailand for what we thought would be only a few months. But that's not what happened. The day he left Hong Kong was the last time I saw him in person. Tristan and I officially divorced in January 2022 after being together for over thirty years.

Our marriage was a casualty of my healing process; I healed while he chose to stay behind. Rather than taking his own healing journey, for him and for us, he said, "I want to set you free." I agreed, without hesitation, the day he spoke those words. I ended our marriage.

Mounting Pressure to Heal

For forty-five years before the focused and intentional part of my healing journey began in June 2020 with my hypnotherapy, the Universe was keeping me under mounting pressure. Like being in a refining fire, I still needed to live through certain events to become who I am and to continue living my life's purpose. But in the process, the Universe was preparing me to heal at the right time once I was ready to do the hard work.

Many of my life events contributed to this pressure, but the fire got scorching hot in 2005 when I was thirty-five. Three significant events occurred within a few weeks of one another. After that, each lived independently in my mind, and fifteen years would pass before I would come to know that these events were not coincidental at all. They were inextricably connected, but at the time they occurred, I had no idea.

The first of those events occurred one night when I was in New York City on a business trip. I got a call from my cousin Jeannine.

"Beth Anne, where are you? Can you talk?" Jeannine was frantic as soon as I answered my cell phone. I immediately heard the scorn and disgust in her voice. I could see the correlating expression on her face as I visualized her on the other end of the phone. I knew something terrible had happened.

"Hi, sure. Yes. I'm in New York, in bed, and just about to turn off the lights. What's wrong?" I replied.

"It's mother. You're not going to believe what she just told us."

"What's wrong with your mom?" I asked, growing increasingly alarmed. *Is she sick? Or worse?* I thought.

"It's disgusting what she said. You remember how we were never allowed to be alone with Nany and Papa when we were kids?"

"Uh, no… not really. I don't recall that," I answered. And I didn't, not then, not now. That hadn't been my experience with them over the years. My parents or some other adults—like my aunt and uncle—were not always present when I was with my grandparents.

"Well, we weren't. And now I know why!" she exclaimed. "Mom just told us that Papa abused her repeatedly when she was growing up. Apparently, that went on for most of her childhood until she and Daddy married. No way in hell our parents were going to let that happen to me, Jeannette, and Deanne. So they always made sure we were never alone with them." Her words were spitting mad. "I'm so disgusted! And if he were still alive, I'd…." Her anger and exasperation were palpable.

My cousins were horrified and shocked by their mother's story. So was I.

We began discussing what each of us remembered about our grandfather and whether we had also been abused. At first, I didn't recall being in the line of his abuse. But at some point, not too long after I heard my aunt's story—I don't recall how long—I had my first memory of being sexually abused by him in that bathroom when I was five. This memory coming to my consciousness is the second significant event that occurred during those weeks.

Around the same time, the third event began when I started having a recurring nightmare. In my nightmare, I was a young child, probably seven or eight years old, wandering through a large, plantation-style, Southern home. The downstairs was open and inviting, set for happy times of family gathering and merriment. A massive kitchen with two huge refrigerators and a large wrought-iron stove sat at one end of the house, giving way to a family dining area, a large parlor, and a family room. In my nightmare, it was Christmastime; the parlor and family room were decorated for the season, reflecting more merriment and joy.

The upstairs scene was very different. In my nightmares, I always climbed the staircase to the right side of a long hallway that spanned the length of the downstairs area. The hallway began with a doorway leading into the kitchen and passed the family room at the other end. As I neared the upstairs landing, I felt the bone chill of a cold and damp place. As I shivered, my nostrils flared as they filled with the musty stench of mildew and mold, the kind that your nose wants to reject because it's so hard to inhale through the stench. Then came the putrid smell of rot and decay, the kind that took my breath away at best but sometimes made me choke and gag as my body felt repulsed.

Finally, I saw the cause of the decay. Creepy crawlies had infested the house, and ghosts were everywhere. Many dead things scattered the staircase landing, as far down the upstairs hallway as I could see. I realized the house and everything in it were dying. Over the years, the environment died more and more. The cold got colder, the stink stank more, the rot got more rotten, and the dead piled up.

In my nightmare, I was acutely aware of the scene and my feelings. I could vividly see the house being haunted, infested, and dying. Yet, despite my young age in the scene, I don't recall being fearful. I just observed what happened over the years in wonderment, but neither the house nor its infestation, dead or alive, touched or scared me.

My nightmare persisted for those fifteen years, unexplained.

Moving to Hong Kong was pivotal to the mounting pressure I was under to heal. Ultimately, I had to shed my marriage to heal and be free, but apparently, the Universe knew that an ocean would need to separate me from Tristan. Only then could I begin to experience life without him.

Hong Kong is also where the people critical to my early healing lived, including my hypnotherapist, my trauma therapist, and the beginnings of my tribe—my support team—who I gathered around me. So that's where the Universe wanted me when my healing journey began.

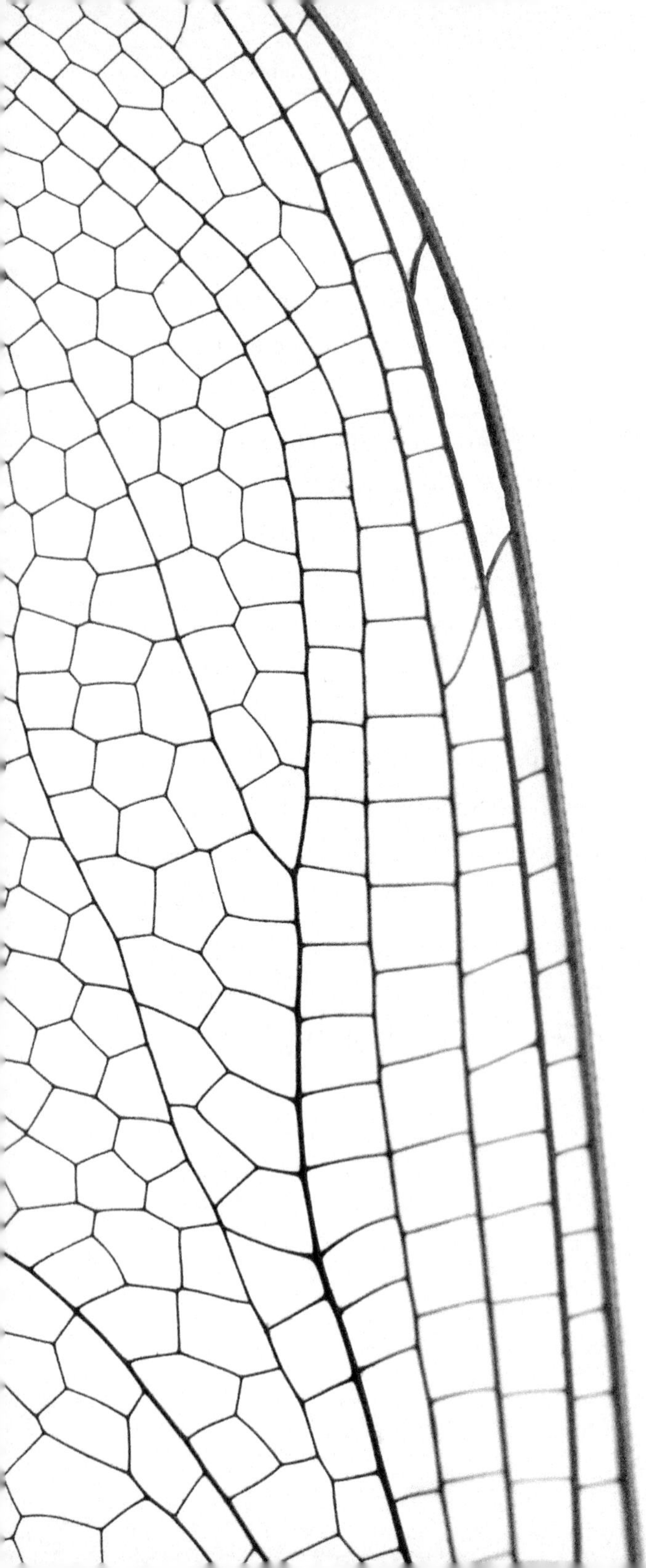

CHAPTER 2

UNCOVERING TRUTHS

ABOUT THREE MONTHS before my hypnotherapy, in April 2020, I took a leadership role at work that required me to connect with my team of 125 people and our clients across Asia in a deeper way than I felt capable of doing. I was responsible for my team's performance and accountable to our clients, both of which required deeper connections for my success.

Before being promoted, my work mainly focused on the project my team was delivering to our client. Yes, I had team members for whom I was responsible and clients to whom I was accountable—sometimes many team members and a lot of client personnel. But the project—the mechanics of uncovering and piecing together the evidence in an investigation—is where I spent 80 percent of my time. Now, suddenly, 80 percent of my time was focused on people and building relationships, whereas only 20 percent of my focus had pointed in that direction previously. I struggled and knew I would continue to struggle without some help.

One day, my medical doctor asked the obligatory question, "So, how are you?"

"I'm alright," I replied unconvincingly.

"Tell me what's going on with you."

"Well, Dr. Nicola, I've taken this new role at work, a leadership role, and I'm worried about my ability to connect with people the way I'm going to need to now. I've always struggled to make deep connections," I explained.

We talked for a few minutes about my struggle, and then she said, "You know, we have a hypnotherapist on staff. I'm hearing good things about how she's helping patients. Seems pretty easy to do things like quit smoking or lose weight. She might be able to help you...."

By then, I had tried so much therapy using different modalities. *What's one more? Why not?* I asked myself. Boy, was I naïve! I thought I was going to hypnotherapy to help me loosen up and forge deeper relationships, and I was utterly unprepared for what came next. I had *no* idea what I was getting into.

Hypnotherapy begins with the therapist establishing a safe spot for you. Think of the safe spot as the portal the therapist takes you through, in and out of the hypnotic state. Count down to hypnosis, and step into your safe spot. Return to your safe spot and count backward up to conscious awareness. This safe spot can also be the place the therapist directs you to if something out of the ordinary happens during the hypnosis, like becoming overly emotional because of something you're experiencing.

My safe spot was a beach. No surprise because the beach is my favorite place on Earth.

As I stepped off the staircase onto my beach, I felt a warm embrace of my five senses. The ocean sparkled under sun rays as the horizon met the azure blue of the cloudless sky. I felt the warm breeze blowing through my hair and against my skin and the sand oozing between my toes. I heard the tranquility of the waves at the water's edge, lapping softly against the shore. I tasted and smelled the salt-sea air as I inhaled deeply, taking in the vast beauty and peace of my beach stretched out in front of me. I felt safe and happy.

In contrast were the dark, ominous, razor-sharp, and jagged cliffs behind me. The staircase I had descended as my therapist counted me down to my subconscious state of awareness—"twenty, nineteen, eighteen, seventeen… two…"—clung to the cliffside. The scene evoked thoughts of a fiery Mordor, or worse, Hell. The peace and tranquility of my beach versus the dark and ominous cliffs were the metaphoric juxtaposition for what I was about to experience—and my life.

As I stepped off the last stair and she finished the countdown, "one," I had entered my hypnotic state. With the first question my hypnotherapist asked, "Beth, why are you here?" I stepped into a house and instantly recognized where I was for the first time ever. I had spent time in that exact house as a kid. My grandparents had worked there at one time. My parents and I visited them in that same house when I was seven or eight. It was that house that had haunted my nightmares for fifteen years.

I don't know why I'm eight years old in my nightmare, given I was younger when my grandfather sexually abused me. Or at least, my younger self is the child who remembers being traumatized by him. Perhaps my dissociation is protecting me from some other trauma I experienced at his hand later in my life. I do have a vague memory of being in the house in reality during one Christmas, but I have no memory of actual interactions with my grandfather, neither good nor bad. Jeannine told me we played hide-and-seek there.

Terrified in my hypnotized state, I cried and trembled uncontrollably as a panic-stricken child would. My terror may have been accurate from when I was young, or it may have been part of my healing process. Either way, my abuser was trying to find me, to hurt me. In my hypnotherapy, I hid under an alcove beneath the same staircase I had climbed all those years in my nightmare. I hid to keep myself safe from him.

"Beth, can you go back to the beach?" my hypnotherapist urged.

"No, he'll see me! He'll hurt me!" I exclaimed, crying out and terrified.

With urgency, my hypnotherapist continued working to keep me safe and get me back to the beach. We worked to extract me from the house and make it go away. After successfully exiting, I found myself playing on a swing set. Although I hadn't remembered that play structure before, I do remember it now in my conscious mind because my cousins and I played there as children.

I was safe outside of the house. I was calmer, catching my breath as my terror released, but just for a fleeting moment. Then, the emotionless aloneness I had experienced as a child surrounded me.

My terror quickly resumed as the hypnotherapy continued because my abuser suddenly opened the door. He was coming out of the house to get me, still wanting to hurt me. As my panic escalated, my hypnotherapist again directed me to my beach. Again, to no avail.

Then, we began working to trap him inside and destroy the house. I mustered my tiny might, pushing against the door, and somehow, given the massive hulk of a man he was, I managed to keep him from getting out of the house. I used the sheer power of my will, which is inherent in my being. But I was unsuccessful in making the house go away, despite my repeated attempts, each one guided by my hypnotherapist.

I tried to make the house disappear with a magic trick. *Poof! You're gone!* I attempted to burn it to the ground to blow away the ashes. Then, I tried to put it inside a balloon and let it float away. I tried to put it in a bubble and pop it, to explode all life from him and the house.

Alas, blowing a bubble around the house and making it levitate ever so slightly off the ground was the best I could do. But the bubble wouldn't float away. Instead, the bubble bobbed up and down, taunting me.

Although I couldn't destroy the house or make it go away, my abuser was locked inside, and the locked house was trapped inside the bubble. Satisfied he couldn't hurt me anymore, my fear calmed. Finally, I returned to the peace and safety of my beach.

My hypnotherapy session had been scheduled for ninety minutes: fifteen minutes to begin and count down to the hypnotic state, plus sixty minutes of hypnotic work, and the last fifteen minutes to come back to the safe place and into conscious awareness. This is the official way it was supposed to happen anyhow. The last fifteen minutes were to be the most important, as I understood it. The patient typically comes safely from the experience and doesn't carry the emotional effects into their everyday life.

My session lasted for three and a half hours. As I was distraught and behaving like a terrified child, my hypnotherapist worked much longer than usual—two extra hours—to help get my emotions under control and bring me back to conscious awareness safely. She kept trying, including all the unsuccessful attempts to destroy the house with my grandfather in it. She wanted to help me leave my fear behind and not bring it back to my conscious awareness.

Even though I left my fear that day in the therapy room, I would face my fear of him soon enough.

I had never understood my nightmare before that day. In fact, despite the remarkably coincidental timing of when my nightmare began and finally having my memory of being abused by my grandfather shortly after the call from my cousin, I had never tied these events together. Nor had I tied either of these events to my Aunt Cheeto telling her daughters about her abuse by the same man. Until that day in the hypnotherapy session, these three events existed separately in my mind. But as I came back to conscious awareness, I knew, for the first time, that all three events were connected.

For forty-five years—despite repeated attempts at unsuccessful couch therapy over the twenty-five years before hypnotherapy, and despite the remarkable events following my aunt telling her story—I never put it together. And…making my story even crazier, I'm a natural-born problem-solver. Professionally, for all those same twenty-five years, I built my expertise as an investigator and factfinder. I find this quite ironic, making me laugh out loud at myself. (Yes, this is probably my inner critic chiding me.)

But I already knew the moment my eyes opened after standing on my beach. Those three events had simmered within me for fifteen years without my awareness of their connection, what it meant for me, and who I was. For the first time, the fragmented threads began to weave together.

From the moment I entered my front door after the session that day, I received almost no support from Tristan. Oddly enough, he was with me in Hong Kong at the time, which was rare in the four years I had lived there by then.

When I came home that day after my hypnotherapy, I doubt anyone would have questioned whether I had been crying or if something was terribly wrong with me. My tears flowed for about five hours through most of the session and into the evening. I'm an ugly crier (this isn't my inner critic being hateful; it's just fact!), so there was no way Tristan didn't see my emotional state when I walked in the door. Yet he met me with an almost unconcerned demeanor, which surprised me. Was I wrong to expect my partner of more than thirty years to show some concern? To ask something like, "Beth, what's the matter? What's happened?" As I told him about my experience, could he not offer something like, "I'm so sorry; we're going to get through this, and you're going to be okay"?

I got none of that. I'm not even sure he hugged me that night. But I do recall his harsh response after I told him what I'd realized that day—that the three separate events in my mind related to my grandfather were all connected.

"Remember that nightmare I've been having? I know what it means," I began, slowly at first. "I know the house. I went there as a kid. It's the same house my grandparents lived and worked in," I explained, my words quickening. "Remember in my nightmare that I was always alone? Well, today, he was in the house with me, searching for me, like we were playing a game of hide-and-seek. I was hiding from him, terrified, because he was trying to hurt me," I continued. "I realized today that my nightmare began when Aunt Cheeto told my cousins about being abused by him," I said, even more hurriedly, as anxiety rushed me through telling him about my discovery. "Do you remember that's also when I had my memory of him touching me? I don't know how, but all of this is related somehow. I'm sure of that. I have this awful feeling in the pit of my stomach that Aunt Cheeto and I might have suffered the same thing!"

"Wow, that explains a lot," he stated coldly.

Of course, that's your response, I thought a split-second after my initial shock. Had he said anything with compassion and love to console me that night, we might have gone on to heal ourselves together. Instead, I would heal myself alone.

That explains a lot. I knew exactly what his statement meant. His response triggered more trauma, taking me back to an earlier time when he had been quite aggressive in expressing his dissatisfaction with our physical intimacy. His harsh words made me feel small and inadequate. They had been layered on top of what I was already giving—all of me—to the chaos of our life and the demands of my career. At the time, I feared he would either divorce me or have an affair—and I was more fearful of the latter. So, I did some things back then to try to "fix me," as if I were the problem. Some of those things perpetuated my unhealthy survivorship.

I realize now I was not "the problem," as there were two of us in that relationship. But I didn't know this then.

After my hypnotherapy, I was in complete shock and bewildered by my realization. *Not one thing about me makes sense*, I told myself. *My life is a lie!!* All put together and polished on the outside, wearing my many disguising masks outwardly, but suddenly full of someone inside who I didn't know. There was a terrified and deeply wounded child in me who I had never met before. I saw her for the first time during the session. *If I don't know myself and whoever that child is, no one likely knows me. After all, how could they?* I was scared of these thoughts.

The lack of support I felt from Tristan during those first few hours after coming home continued—exacerbating my already raw feelings. Somehow, what was happening to me became entirely about him.

This is when it first hit me: *He can't see anyone other than himself, including me.* I didn't consider this in a judgmental or vindictive way, but I began the process of seeing him, *really* seeing him for who—and how—he was.

I can now understand who he was and his response to me because I've done the work to understand my trauma. But in those early days, his completely unhelpful responses only inflicted more trauma on me.

Also during this time, emotions—of all sorts—began to return after years of suppression. They flowed, and not in a great way. I would vacillate between deep sadness and full-on rage. Not directed at anyone, my emotions, which needed to come out, were unleashed.

My sadness was a deep, sometimes visceral wailing. While my tears flowed uncontrollably, sometimes for long periods, no words came because I couldn't describe the source of my emotion. Instead, there was a deep, painful place in my core—an early identification of the tightly bound constraint over my heart that I would soon discover. I was beginning to let go of long-held grief for the wounded child in me whom I had never known.

As the realization that my grandfather had hurt me set in, I was angry at him for what he had done. Although I didn't have the appreciation I now have for the severity of his abuse, I knew from the events of the hypnotherapy session that he had been someone who headlined my pain. The lies my brain had stored about him were suddenly revealed, and my thoughts began to unravel that pain. *How dare you? You were supposed to love me! You were supposed to protect me. But instead, you used your power over me and took advantage of me as a small child just because you could! What sort of a cruel, twisted monster are you?*

Over the years, when my emotions had all but ceased flowing, I lived behind a tall, thick wall I'd built around myself. I believe what Tristan saw, however, was stability, a rock, a problem-solver who didn't get derailed by emotion, regardless of the situation. So when I went into this phase of uncontrollable emotion-letting—and complex emotions—he was completely confused, probably threatened, and had no idea how to respond to me. He went so far as to tell me I was *scaring him* as if I was letting my emotions go intentionally at him. Yet still, he did not attempt to connect with me in a way that might have consoled or helped me.

After a couple of weeks, because I wasn't getting the support I needed at home, and since I wanted to be alone to process my thoughts, I checked myself into a hotel—alone.

I specifically chose the hotel because of its nearby park and bird aviary, which was beautiful and peaceful. It remains one of my favorite places in Hong Kong. I spent countless hours in that aviary after my hypnotherapy session, usually deep in my thoughts and trying to make sense of my life over the months that followed. I left a lot of tears, sadness, and anger with the birds in that park.

I was drawn to the aviary because it's filled with enormous trees that occupy the entire space under the top of the enclosure. A suspended walkway courses through the tops of the trees, so I literally had a bird's-eye view of the stunning creatures with their bright colors and varied headdresses formed from their feathers. There are so many different species from various parts of Asia, each beautiful in its unique way. I loved to sit and observe the birds flitting about. Under my watch, they discovered something to eat, sometimes went through mating rituals, other times built nests, and even occasionally taught a fledgling to fly. Even under the enclosure of the aviary, the birds lived as though they were carefree. I reveled in their freedom.

I wrestled with my thoughts about my grandfather over the first ten-day period I spent with the birds. *Really? He did that to me? Did he touch me like that? Is that what he did to Aunt Cheeto? My nightmare has been trying to tell me this for all these years? Why have I never put this together before now? Do I even believe it?... But what else could my nightmare mean? And the timing with Aunt Cheeto telling her girls can't be a coincidence, can it?... I'm not that child who was loved and doted on, who led that idyllic life. Everything about who I believed myself to be is a lie. If my life is a lie, who am I?*

As I wrestled with my thoughts, I increasingly needed to talk about what I was experiencing. The people I first turned to were two women in Hong Kong who are still part of my tribe. We were all professional colleagues working together who had become good friends socially. We'd begun to share deeper parts of who we were and what was happening in our lives, but the depth of our relationships was about to change dramatically.

I invited my girlfriends, Sally and Kate, to my hotel for dinner one night. Afterward, we sat in the hotel lobby, chit-chatting about nothing important as I got the courage to tell them what was happening. I knew they sensed immediately that something was very wrong with me. But they waited—patiently, lovingly—for me to open and hold my first real conversation ever about the deepest parts of *me*. Parts I hadn't consciously known about myself just two weeks before.

That night, I was scared to tell them about the hypnotherapy and what I had pieced together so far. *Will they think I'm weird for going to hypnotherapy?* I wondered. *Will they find it too far out and unbelievable? Some woo-woo or hocus-pocus kind of a thing?* Oddly enough, that night, I became more concerned about the possible answers to that question rather than their reaction to what I had discovered during the session.

I also wondered, *What will they think about me being touched by my grandfather in that way? Will they believe me? Will they think I am damaged, or worse, not fit to be friends* with anymore? Will they dismiss what I tell them? Will they abandon me?

I was also embarrassed and worried about what they would think about me after I shared. *They think I'm this badass, an expert, all put together and on top of her game. After I tell them, I'll be like a wilted flower.* What will they think when they see me crumbling? Will they think I'm weak for crying so much? Will they think I've completely lost my mind?! Will Sally and Kate ever want to work with me again?

I didn't know what I would tell them or what my words would be. But as I shared my story, they were so kind, gentle, accepting, and loving.

"What's going on?" Sally finally asked me. "Something's wrong. I can see it on your face. And you're fidgeting." She looked at me with the inquisitive expression I had come to know of her professionally.

"I'm nervous and scared to tell you, but I must get this out. You're the only two people I feel comfortable telling. But I'm scared. Please don't think I'm weird or crazy."

"No one is going to think you're weird or crazy," Kate said. "Whatever it is, it's okay, and we're here for you."

"OK. Here we go…. I did this thing a few days ago. I went to hypnotherapy."

"*Hypnotherapy?* Why? What was that like?" Sally asked.

"Oh, that's interesting. I've never tried that before," Kate replied. "Yeah, what was that like?"

"Terrifying! One of the worst experiences of my life. And I think I'm cracking up. Maybe I'm going crazy!"

"What happened?" they both asked, almost in unison.

I told them about recognizing the house in my nightmare for the first time and my ensuing battle to eradicate my grandfather and the house. I told them how terrified I had literally been, physically, as I lay on the table during the session. They both looked at me incredulously but with deep concern.

"It was so awful what happened. What I saw was so scary. But what I've started to realize and piece together about my life is the part that's *really* terrifying to me." I told them about my subsequent realization when I opened my eyes that there was no coincidence in the timing of my Aunt Cheeto telling her daughters about being abused by my grandfather and the other two events that occurred around the same time.

"I know my grandfather touched me inappropriately. That seems very real now; it is real. But it seems like my mind had erased it all until now," I told them in a quandary. "My mind seems to have erased most of my memories." I went on to explain the vast voids in my memory of my life, even monumental events for which I had no recorded memory.

"Oh my, that sounds really awful, and I'm so sorry that you went through that," Kate said in her compassionate way. "There's a lot going on there. You never knew about this?"

"Yes. And no. I guess…it's like all of this sat in the back of my mind, and now, for some reason, it's all coming together. It all has to be linked together more than I realize. There's some greater connection. I feel it in my gut," I explained as best I could. "But that's not the worst of it. The worst part is realizing I don't know who I am, which feels awful. I feel like my entire life has been a lie!" I confided. Tears streamed down my cheeks as I uttered the words.

Because of Sally's work experience, she told me two things that night that were pivotal to my healing journey.

"Beth, you know I did some work early in my career prosecuting the creeps who abuse children, right? I think we've talked about this." In the early days of her career, Sally was a criminal prosecutor, working on child sexual abuse cases.

"Oh, yes, you've told me that before," I responded with trepidation.

"You know that's how we got Marissa, right?" Marissa is Sally's adopted daughter. "Well, anyway, your memory loss sounds like dissociation because you're traumatized. You're sick, and you need help."

"What do you mean?" I asked in confusion.

"What you've described, your grandfather 'touching you,' that's sexual abuse. Your memory loss? That sounds like dissociation. And what happened during the hypnotherapy is that your brain is probably starting to process what you've been through. You need to find a specialist, someone trained in child sexual abuse and trauma, to help you with this," Sally explained. "And the memory loss you have, that happens when traumatized people dissociate from what they're experiencing. If you don't remember so much of your life, I'm sorry to say this, but there might be more."

"Oh, dear God! This is horrible," Kate exclaimed, stating the obvious. "What can we do to help you? Anything you need, ask."

"I mean what I've said with love, Beth, not criticism. I'm really concerned about you," Sally said reassuringly.

"Yes, we love you!" Kate agreed. "And you're going to get through this. We're going to help you."

Abuse? Trauma? Dissociation? A bewildered *Whaaaaaaat the fuuuu…?!* is precisely how I felt that night. But at the same time, I heard words that began to help me understand what I had experienced throughout my life. Suddenly, I felt a modicum of hope where there was none, only a moment before. I'll never forget the extremes of what I felt that night. Bewildered, confused, and scared, but strange for me, also unconditionally loved. In those moments, I felt like someone cared about me and only me.

These two women became my rocks throughout my healing journey, and every day, I thank the Universe for them in my life. I couldn't have made it through the hardest parts without them. What they taught me about love is immeasurable. But what they did for me in those immediate days after my hypnotherapy session was miraculous. Hypnotherapy was my gateway to healing, but talking to them that night helped me take the first tactical steps forward on my healing pathway.

Many beautiful examples of my healing journey unfolding before me happened that night and for about eighteen months afterward. I'll tell you about some of these as I share my story, but this next one relates to my insatiable thirst for knowledge.

Immediately after talking to Sally and Kate, I was curious about trauma, but more so about the trauma response and how we cope as survivors. Somehow, I knew this would help me to understand what had happened and what was happening to me as a survivor. So I started reading. This is how I began to see what I refer to as my *unhealthy survivorship*. I also began to see many of the stones that had gone into building the wall I was living behind.

People who were healed lived in the books I read. Many of their stories showed trauma and trauma responses, but they were also about healing. I quickly realized I, too, could heal, which impacted me profoundly. Upon realizing this, I quickly shifted into a mode of rejecting my unhealthy survivorship.

Suddenly, I considered it complete bullshit to live burdened by the heavy weight of my past, trapped behind my wall—all because other people had taken advantage of me, abused me, and abandoned me. Like a coat of tar and feathers stuck to me, I *really, really* wanted to shake it off. I remember literally shaking my body and saying in group therapy, "Get this shit off of me!"

That's exactly what I went on to do.

My hypnotherapy session is my most traumatic but enlightening experience ever. That session held the moment when I began my awareness of having been sexually abused as a child. At the same time, that moment marked my gateway to healing.

Since that day, I've been on my intentional and focused healing journey to break down my wall.

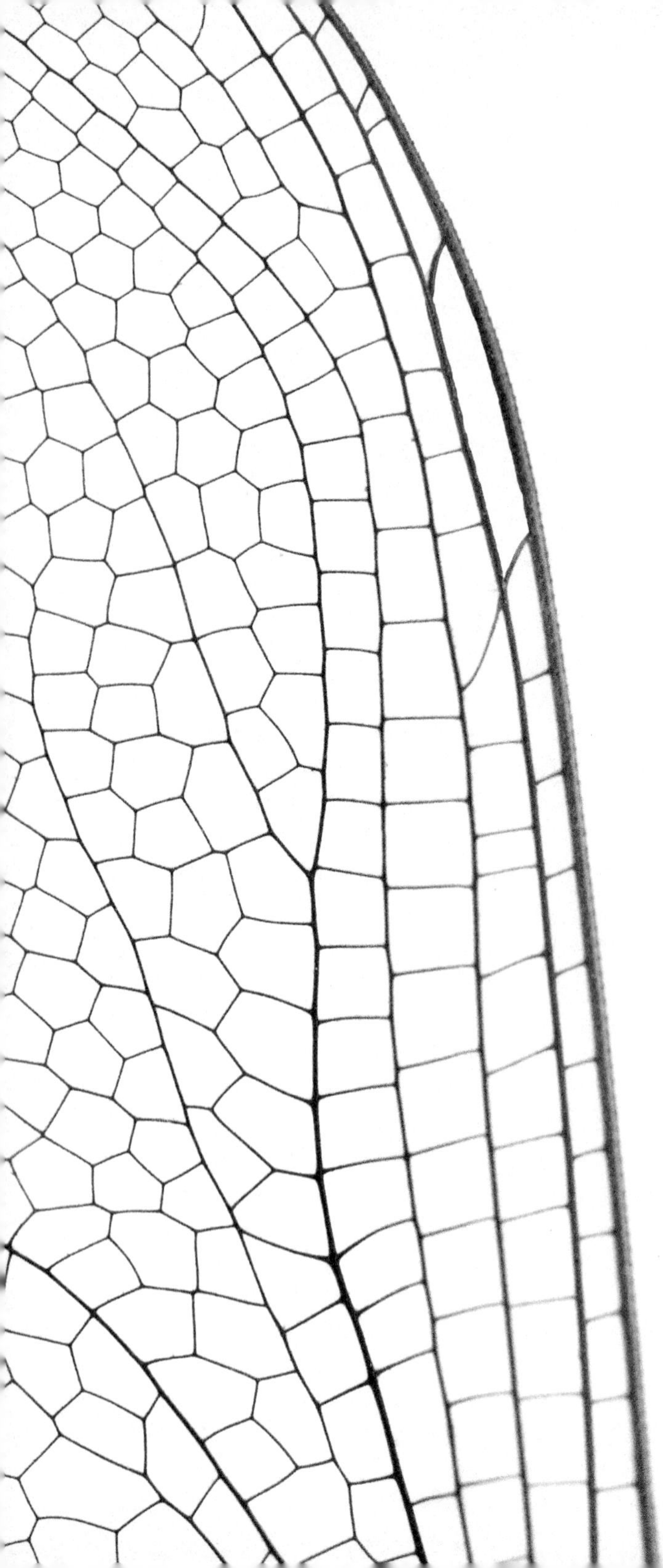

CHAPTER 3

ACKNOWLEDGING WALLS

I LIVED FAR too many years behind the wall I had built to protect myself from the trauma and abuse others inflicted on me. Some of those people who hurt me should have protected me, but they didn't. Others represented passing relationships with those who never cared about my well-being. In the moment, they only considered what they wanted. In some cases, what I survived occurred in a single moment, but in other cases, the pain not only blindsided me but continued over many years.

I also suffered from my hurtful actions against myself—my trauma responses and unhealthy survivorship.

With each experience, both trauma and survival layered on top of me—event by event, year after year. As a result, my wall grew and grew. When I discovered it post-hypnotherapy, it was forty-five years tall and forty-five years thick. Trapped behind it, I was alone and lonely.

How I lived my life—the elements of being in survival mode behind my wall—are described in this chapter. I'll tell you in my own words while associating common clinical terms where relevant. I knew nothing about some of this when I was trapped behind my wall. Other parts I could explain conceptually, but I had no idea they were these clinical terms associated with *my* trauma responses. I'm much more knowledgeable now, so I can use today's standard terms to explain better how I lived.

Dissociation

Five years of age is very young to have been sexually abused for the first time. I remember the event vividly as if it were recorded in my mind like a movie, and I'm right back there when I think about it. That memory is so vivid that I can smell the foul stench of my perpetrator's cigar-laden breath, mixed with his body odor emanating as if he hadn't bathed after several days of toiling in the hot summer sun. For a survivor, that depth of memory causes a reliving of the trauma.

That may be the only time I was sexually abused as a child, but I don't know for sure because I suffer from dissociation. My dissociation began that day when my grandfather abused me. I have almost no recorded memories for the rest of my childhood and fuzzy memories, at best, of my early adult years. Even milestone events in my life, like my sixteenth birthday, high school graduation, and wedding, aren't recorded in my mind. I cannot relive being in any of those places or times. It's as if someone took an eraser to the whiteboard of my mind and wiped it clean. Most of what I know about those days comes from photographs and stories people have told me.

Dissociation also showed up—sometimes still does—during conversations with someone attacking or rejecting me emotionally. The recorder of my mind stops, even though I'm fully engaged in the conversation. Even moments later, I hold no recollection of what we talked about. This phenomenon makes it hard to explain to someone what they said exactly to hurt me. I can't remember the details, but I can remember how they made me feel.

Discovering the words *dissociation* and *dissociative amnesia* formed some of my first moments of being touched by the Universe during my healing. In these moments, I've literally felt the Universe, perhaps the hand of God, reaching out and touching me with an awakening. Strength and knowledge emanate from a being who looks like an archangel in my mind, beaming protection over me and my spirit through love. That's what it feels like. And I'm filled with excitement and jubilation at the experience each time. I call these "Universe touches."

I've had many of these moments as I've healed, though now they tend to be epiphanies that make the hair on my arms stand up rather than a jubilant feeling of excitement. I guess I've come to expect them now as markers of progress on my healing journey—a Higher Power continuing to lead me.

For years, I was desperately curious about why I didn't have memories like other people. In the curious way we do, I would query others to try and understand how their memories worked and what they saw in their mind's eyes when they remembered.

"Do you remember the day you graduated from high school? Right now, are you back in the moment? In your mind's eye, can you see yourself there that day, as it was when you experienced it? Do you remember what you were wearing? Do you remember who sat on either side of you as you waited to cross the stage?"

"What about your wedding day? Do you need the video to remind you, or is it recorded in your mind? Do you remember walking down the aisle?"

I had none of those memories, so I marveled at people who could see themselves there in the moment, even something that happened to them thirty, forty, fifty, sixty years ago. Yes, some details may have faded over time, but generally, they seemed to be present with the subject and time of their memories.

I never understood why mine were gone until I began to read about survivorship. Eventually, this made sense to me, and now I believe dissociation has been my brain's way of protecting me. Some survivors have vivid memories of what happened to them, but for some reason, that wasn't my brain's choice. I trust my brain, so I don't go searching for what is hidden. I don't need to know those facts about my life to heal, and I don't need the triggers. I also believe at least part of the reason why my brain chose dissociation over recording my trauma was to prevent me from being so damaged that I was unable to heal.

Knowing that dissociation is normal for trauma survivors was hugely beneficial to my understanding of my survivorship. Something finally made sense. I didn't feel so alone because I realized *I'm not the only one; there are so many of us with this condition that the experts have officially labeled it.*

Substance Abuse

My alcohol and drug use began when I was in high school and gradually worsened through my early adult years. Part of my substance abuse came from trying to fit in with the crowd in my early years. I was trying to make "BJ" a cool kid in high school. But as I got older and my trauma piled on, it became about coping, escaping, and trying to feel something while also numbing the pain—particularly the pain that came from some of my interactions with my parents and Tristan. Perhaps alcohol and drugs were another form of dissociation.

I escaped this survival mechanism when the crowd I ran with began to get into criminal activity. Staying one step ahead of the law to protect illegal gambling rings went on for several months, culminating in our business partner and supposed "friend" ordering a hit on a local county sheriff who was just trying to uphold the law. That "friend" supplied a lot of the drugs, but ordering the hit on another person's life was a deal-breaker for me in our relationship. It scared me out of the "friendship" and scared me out of the drugs.

Fortunately for me, when I decided to stop using these substances, I could. *Pick it up, put it down* is in my DNA, and I do not have an addictive personality, thankfully—perhaps another gift from the Universe. Drugs have been gone from my life for a long time. But even today, if I'm ever in the depth of dealing with a hurtful relationship, alcohol could be a problem if I allowed it to be.

My Family in Exile

I was estranged from my parents for many years of my adulthood, continuing for a while post-hypnotherapy. During the years of my estrangement, if anyone asked about my parents, I went through a painful and contorted explanation, painstakingly clarifying that the decision to estrange was mine and not theirs. "Just to be clear, I'm not the family's black sheep," I insisted. "I decided to estrange from my family. It was my choice to walk away, not their choice to cast me out."

Natalie and her kids, my nephew and two nieces, were included in the people I exiled. So, too, were my extended family. None of this was about choosing sides. Instead, when I became estranged from my parents, I stepped out of all their lives. I had no need to make anyone feel like they had to choose sides, nor was I trying to punish my parents (or other family members) in any way. I just wanted peace from what had become a highly toxic environment while interacting with my parents—my mom, in particular.

My mom and I fought a lot when I was a young adult after my parents repatriated to the US. She would argue that my feelings I didn't understand and couldn't explain were wrong (feelings are never right or wrong, by the way), and we would end up in screaming matches. Even in public. Our interactions were emotionally unsafe for both of us, and I chose to step away from the toxicity.

Many families are burdened by dysfunction, and mine is no different. Our dysfunction comes from all of us being survivors of traumatic human-to-human experiences, including with our parents. I know more today about my dad's experiences than I did when I exiled my family, and I continue to learn about my mother's as we work to heal our relationship. None of us are alone in survivorship.

I must highlight how my parents' experiences manifested in my life, ultimately playing a significant role in creating my wall. I chose the following example because it will become relevant later when discussing my healing evolution and exploration of love. This shows how my home environment wasn't a safe space when I was a teenager, during a time when I could have been learning to develop healthy intimate relationships with males. Not only was I not learning about this, but I was also learning a solid lesson on how to isolate myself—estrange myself—from my parents.

Several factors contributed to my home not being a safe space to learn how to develop healthy intimate relationships. This dynamic reflected my parents' experiences and how they lived then.

First, sex in my immediate family was a taboo subject and a topic seldom (or maybe never) discussed. Looking back now, I can see that my dad was trying to shield me from anything that looked like sexual abuse. His reasons are obvious now because my dad is a cycle breaker. In fact, the greatest gift he ever gave to me, and the one I'm most grateful for, is that he never sexually abused me. I shudder to think how messed up my life could have been if he had perpetuated onto me the generational curse that plagued our family.

Second, I was raised in a home where strict Christian values and teachings were ever-present. I was taught that sex out of wedlock is a sin. My expected behavior from this teaching was "just don't do it." But that was it. To my recollection, that was the extent of talking about it with my parents.

I was also taught that sex out of wedlock, with heaven forbid a baby made, would disrespect the family and disgrace their name. Ironic, isn't it? My grandfather's behavior was buried for so many years, yet the message remained: *do not tarnish the family name by getting pregnant.*

My first sexual relationship was during my first year of college. Mostly, it was a healthy relationship, although he was an upperclassman who may have seen me as a conquest. I never told my parents anything about that young man. They were living far away from me for the entirety of that relationship, which meant there was never an opportunity for them to meet. I never did tell them about him.

It wasn't until my junior year of college, after I had been dating Tristan for some time that my mother initiated a conversation one day. Out of the blue, she asked me, "Are you having sex with him?" Her reaction to my "Yes" answer was exasperation and disappointment. That made me feel like a sinner. Like I was doing something wrong, even though I loved him and my inner knowing knew we were headed for marriage and a life together. I don't recall discussing with my mother how I *felt* about him or whether I loved or would marry him.

After that, they showed no genuine attempt to accept him, nor did he try to accept my parents. All three of them got in the way of any bonding, but I had expected more from my parents for my sake. The divide between them became a contributing factor to my exiling my parents. It was easy for them to part ways and easier for me to choose Tristan over them because I didn't feel the pull of a bond with either parent sufficient to keep me from walking away.

The other factor at play was that my dad's reaction to me dating a boy in high school was to tease me. He would make fun of me, almost bullying me. "Bethie's got a boyfriend, Bethie's got a boyfriend," he'd tease in a singing voice that made me recoil in embarrassment. I felt shame. Whenever I had the chance *not* to tell my parents about a relationship, I felt relief.

Because of how my dad made me feel—small and inadequate—I never lasted more than a couple of weeks dating someone. I had plenty of opportunities and short-term relationships. Still, as soon as my parents learned about any new boy, my dad's teasing would drive me to end the connection almost immediately. Even if the teasing hadn't begun, but a situation was developing into something they might discover, I would end it. Sadly, not one of those boys ever knew why. I'm not even sure I knew why back then. Now I see my reaction was merely avoiding an inevitably unbearable situation with my dad.

When I put my parents in exile, I had no foundation to lean on to understand what was happening to *them*. I only felt the deep pain of emotional neglect, which sometimes felt like outright rejection or abandonment, as I tried to express any of my feelings as an adult. I had rarely expressed my feelings as a child, and doing so didn't get easier as I got older. My pain from our human-to-human interaction had been building for many, many years by the time I made my decision. I desperately wanted my pain to stop, and I saw exile as the only path forward.

Emotionless

Over the years, behind my wall, I became mostly emotionless. I've had the good fortune to reclaim my relationship with my parents recently. More about this to come, but one of the benefits of reconnecting has been talking about what happened to me and how it impacted me. Of course, the initial abuse by my grandfather when I was so young has had a fair amount of conversation, particularly with my dad because it was his father. "Why didn't you tell me?" my dad asked me not so long ago. "I don't know, Dad. What exactly does a five-year-old say about something like that?" He shrugged and raised his eyebrows in a silent acknowledgment of the truth.

But my mom recognized that I was emotionless from an early age. Recently, she told me that when she looks back at pictures of me as a child, she can see I almost never smiled. Sad, but another truth. Photographs don't lie. I had already withdrawn inside of myself.

I don't remember much about my life through my early twenties, mainly because of my dissociative amnesia, so I cannot say much about my emotions in those years. I made many friends in college who remember our good times together, so I must have had some joy then. But before, in high school, I'm not so sure. Growing up internationally, we were somewhat transient with our relationships anyhow, but high school is also when I again suffered sexual abuse, coupled with bullying and betrayal. None of my friends seemed to care, and because of my dad's teasing around boys, I didn't feel safe telling my parents. I was isolated and alone in dealing with that trauma, which I'm sure also contributed to me being emotionless.

As an adult in my thirties and early forties, I went through a few years where deep sadness flowed freely from me. I sobbed uncontrollably, triggered by what seemed like silly things—like a TV or movie scene wherein a father and daughter, or husband or wife, were lovingly hugging one another after a heartfelt conversation. Back then, I had no idea why I sobbed; suddenly, my tears would just flow. Embarrassed, I would rush to wipe them away. And pray, *God, please don't let me cry in public!*

This was also the time during which most discussions with my mother would end in a fight, leaving me to feel that my emotions were wrong. I never talked about what I experienced or felt with my dad. And I didn't know how to share my feelings with Tristan. I'm not sure how he would have responded anyhow, given who he is and how he responded to me in those days and weeks after my hypnotherapy session.

Then, as I got older and my wall grew, my emotions mostly quit flowing. Occasionally, I could be provoked to a major outburst of anger if someone—my mother or Tristan—made me angry. I was like a human volcano, quiet outside but rumbling inside until something would cause me to erupt. A handful of times, losing a beloved pet made me very sad, but I rarely experienced joy. Mostly, I stuffed my emotions into little boxes that became stones in my wall.

I recall the feelings of happiness and joy were situational and momentary, like when Tristan and I raced in the Big Bend Open Road Race in the early 2000s. The car race was on a highway between two small towns in West Texas—near Big Bend National Park—where a sixty-mile stretch of road closed to everyone except the racers. Anyone could enter the race with any car so long as the vehicle's safety modifications met the requirements for the speed class entered. We raced there and back across the sixty miles with the goal of maintaining an exact speed over the entire course. The winner in each speed class was the car closest to maintaining the speed end-to-end. For example, one second over or under maintaining 110 mph, our speed class, and you wouldn't win. We were something like ten seconds off the perfect time for a 120-mile race. It was no small feat to be perfect, but our plus-ten seconds meant placing fourteenth, as I recall.

The few hours of the race itself were exhilarating and a lot of fun. And I've seen a picture of me smiling inside our car. This is one of the few memories partially recorded in my mind from this period, but the before and after were flanked by the typical chaos of my married life.

Busyholics in Chronic Chaos

I suffered from the demands and madness of my life. At the same time, I struggled to meet Tristan's expectations of me. To be fair, I'm guessing he would say the same thing about suffering from the chaos and demands of our lives. As if getting from East Texas to West Texas with our race car in tow on a flatbed trailer and competing in the race wasn't enough, we also had two young puppies with us—Australian shepherds. They were demanding in their care and training, and we were trying to keep consistency for them. Anything that didn't meet Tristan's expectations, I felt through his reactions and ensuing actions toward me, and it was always my fault. I constantly sensed his dissatisfaction and disappointment, often through the way he looked at me with what felt like contempt. I was perpetually in a mode of going, doing with *everything* I had in me to make **everything** okay—always trying to meet his expectations and keep him happy, striving to avoid an irrational reaction. Racing and caring for two young puppies, I got no physical rest, and dealing with Tristan was emotionally exhausting.

Our car in the race was an almost new, pristine, candy-apple-red Fiftieth Anniversary edition Corvette Z06. I was afraid of damaging the car. Afraid of Tristan's inevitable anger and visible display of disappointment should it be damaged even in the slightest of ways. Ironically, I was the one working to provide the means to buy the car. So, I should have been able to enjoy it as much as he did. But I rarely drove it, even though I loved the thrill of running through the gears and feeling the car's aerodynamics at high speed when it drew down and embraced the road like an old friend.

My fear extended into ensuring the car made it out to West Texas unharmed while tied down on the flatbed trailer. Ensuring we, including the puppies, had everything we needed for the trip and race can only be described as chaos. Chaos in the packing, so as not to forget even one thing. Chaos in our truck, trailer, and race car moving down the road. Chaos in fulfilling the racing requirements and maintenance of the vehicle. Chaos in taking care of the dogs. Chaos in taking care of Tristan. Chaos if anything went even slightly awry, as Tristan's emotions would show it.

I tell that story because it highlights some excitement in my life. But it came at a price. That kind of chaos was my norm for about twenty-five years. While I worked my full-time, demanding job—first as an independent financial statement auditor and then as a forensic accountant investigating white-collar crime and developing into a business leader and mentor—I also worked a full-time, demanding job on our mini-ranches.

And making all those moves of our mini-ranch added to the chaos. Each was laden with its own micro traumas. We were never finished moving. The land *always* had some need—to tend the pasture or repair the endless things that needed mending. I've fixed barbed-wire fences at night by truck headlights more times than I care to remember. And at times, we had many, many animals to care for. There must have been eighty at the highest headcount, including dogs, cats, cows, goats, horses, chickens, ducks, geese, and the servals.

I experienced a lot of death with our animals, some with the normal expiration of life, others tragically. I agonized in gut-wrenching pain the day I helped my miniature schnauzer, Rosco, cross the rainbow bridge at an old age. He was the son I never had. And the horse I learned to ride on died unexpectedly of a flesh-eating fungus, phycomycosis. Dakota's death never left me.

Then there was my Egyptian Mau cat, Sebastian, whom Tristan shot because Sebastian was a "killer." Tristan fed the wild birds and squirrels, and our fowl and their babies were free-range on our property. There's the natural order in the animal world, and Sebastian was a predator, sometimes killing the wild birds, squirrels, and our fowl. There was irony in Tristan killing Sebastian and pain for me.

Steele, my beloved Australian shepherd, was killed tragically and viciously by Bambi, the pit bull owned by our caretaker in Conifer. When we allowed Bambi to move in with her, I knew of the risk that our two dogs would fight because I had seen them interacting. But in my desperation to move to Hong Kong, I ignored the warning signs, and Steele paid the ultimate price. I was devastated by her death.

All the macro and micro traumas made us busyholics in chronic chaos. Rarely, if ever, was there rest from the demands of our life. We created much of our own suffering and never found peace.

Self-Isolation and Repression

While I didn't know it at the time, I began to lose myself that day when I was first abused as a young child. First came the dissociation. Then came my long marriage wherein I gave everything I had to Tristan—emotionally, financially, mentally, and physically. I kept very little for myself, and for many years, any form of self-care was nonexistent. I even gave up something as simple as listening to music, which I loved, because he did not like music generally, and certainly not the music I liked. Giving it up meant I wouldn't think about it, which was easier than arguing. I wouldn't risk being disappointed repeatedly by his resistance.

I also gave up going to movies that I would have enjoyed. I saw a small number of blockbusters on the big screen—*Titanic*, *Lord of the Rings* trilogy, and *Avatar*—but I could tell he was miserable and didn't want to be there. That extended even to watching movies at home. So we rarely did. But one of the benefits of traveling as much as I did for work is the phenomenal and current movie selection airlines offer. I had plenty of time on long-hauls worldwide and cross-country domestic flights, so I'm not totally void of movie trivia these days!

I also gave up being creative or doing any artwork, including painting, needlework, or crafts. This one gets to the core of who I am and who I gave up for far too many years. I've learned I am creative and analytical—dual-brained, left and right-side active. This is why I did so well professionally—always analytical around the facts but using innovative methods to track down the unique ways people commit fraud. Artwork, particularly painting, feeds my soul through the expression of myself and my emotions.

Shopping with girlfriends, getting a massage, or some other pampering never happened. Getting my hair and nails done was only about maintenance and professional image, not self-care for the benefit of my well-being or to enjoy time together with my sister or a friend. I gave up most activities that contributed to *me*.

I gave up my family—a "familyectomy," if you will indulge me—and my friends. This especially applied to family and friends who I really needed as part of my support team. Tristan didn't like them, and letting them go was easier than fighting. Sure, my past trauma with my parents made distancing myself from them easy.

In our "spare time," our extracurricular activities mostly represented what interested Tristan—prioritizing the animals and land, car racing, motocross racing, horses and rodeoing, snowboarding, and so on. I tried to get into everything that interested him, hoping I would find sustained fulfillment, but I never did. Joy never came. Instead, I felt disappointed, compounded by the stress of the preparation and logistics of getting to wherever we were going. Often, the process was just hard; sometimes, we experienced more chaos.

Car racing probably came the closest to bringing me joy, though it, too, was rife with chaos beyond the racing experience. Motocross racing was like car racing in terms of the chaos before and after the events, although I didn't have the same fear of damaging the bikes as I had with the Corvette. I did enjoy pushing myself to see what I could do on the bike. Snowboarding isn't my thing, and I'm *definitely* a beach girl, not a snow bunny.

I suppose losing myself, too, may be another manifestation of my dissociation, my escape. But the toll on me was tremendous. I survived many years being mostly alone, separated from people who would have enriched my life. Much of the time in those early years with Tristan was good, but even that relationship eventually became about running the business of our life together, not about emotional support.

And I always felt like I was his last priority, ranking third or fourth, somewhere behind him, land, animals, and other things. He cried when he sold his race car—not the Corvette, but another car he had raced as an amateur—to provide the cash we needed to recover from our hemorrhage after our Myrtle Springs, Combine, Kaufman debacle. He also cried at selling "his cows" when we moved from Texas to Colorado, although he chose to live in a part of Colorado where the terrain wasn't suited for raising cattle. Then he cried as he considered losing the land he loved so much in Colorado because of our pending divorce.

He also cried when each of the servals died. The last one who passed was Princess, whom he adored. I have a photo of the two of them, my greatest reminder today of how much he loved her. The look on his face, a look I have never seen directed at me, is deep devotion. But I never saw him cry over me, not even as our marriage ended and our lives parted ways.

I had no tribe, so I felt utterly alone and lonely behind my wall.

Why would I choose Tristan over my family and friends? I've asked myself this question occasionally as I've coursed through my healing journey, always foregoing the work to answer. *It doesn't matter*, I would say to myself dismissively. But it *does* matter. It matters because I don't want to make the same mistake again as I continue my journey to know true love. So, I will attempt to answer that question.

Part of the answer lies in the human condition of being trauma survivors, which Tristan and I shared. I think we were drawn and held together by an unconscious understanding of each other's pain and suffering. From the first day we met, we had no idea we were both trauma survivors and no idea we both needed to heal. Because we had never healed, our unhealthy survivorship perpetuated more trauma for both of us throughout our marriage.

I drove on our first date. Otherwise, I would have ridden on the back of his off-road motorbike. His mother had recently taken back his car, which she had gifted him, because she needed money for something or other. That type of behavior from her was ever-present. Putting herself and her needs before those of her child meant he went without for much of his life before me. Even providing basic childcare needs for him, like getting your kid to school and ensuring he had food, was scarce. From an early age, Tristan got himself to school by seeing where the hands were on the clock, even before he could tell time, and on many days, school was the only place where he ate.

I met his father only twice in all our years together. I could sit beside him today, and he would have no idea who I am.

Another reason I chose Tristan over my family and friends is that our relationship fed my need to be a caregiver. However, my caregiving turned into rescuing, and I suffered as his rescuer. Rescuing him meant I always prioritized him and gave him space to do whatever he needed or wanted. I put myself aside, hiding behind my wall, for him.

I also deeply value commitment, and I'm an eternal optimist. When I commit to someone, I'm entirely in. Therefore, it took me a while to accept that my marriage had served its purpose and was no longer fulfilling my highest and best good. My commitment kept me in the marriage twice as long as I probably should have stayed, although the story of my life—the story written in this book—meant that I had to stay. All those years, optimism gave me hope for a better tomorrow.

Lost Behind My Wall

During every waking moment, I gave to some other living being or thing—except myself. My state of being wasn't something I consciously considered. Rather, I was just always focused on someone or something else.

Demands on my time started when Tristan and I first began dating in college. I lived in my fraternity house back then. (I'm a member of the Chi Omega Women's Fraternity, the first sorority established before the word "sorority" was coined, so we're a "women's fraternity.") Whenever I needed to stop by the house to pick up something while on our way to somewhere else, usually his house, he would wait for me outside. Other girls' boyfriends would go inside and wait for them, socializing with others in the house for however long it took, but not Tristan.

When I was in the fraternity house, I was on a time limit for no reason at all other than that he didn't want to wait for me. He'd point at the clock in the car as we parked, and as I opened the car door to exit, he'd say, "It's 6:54. I'm leaving at 7:04, with or without you." I acquiesced, hurriedly doing whatever I needed, with little time to engage or bond with my fraternity sisters and receive any emotional nurturing from them.

Being treated that way was painful enough, but do you know the real kicker? We were in *my* car. My car, not his! Yet I said nothing against his demand. Not even, "Okay, I'll take you home first and then come back." Instead, I just complied and obeyed. In that way, from the very beginning of our relationship, I was telling him how he treated me was okay and reinforcing his power over me. I relinquished my voice.

Those kinds of demands continued as I worked my two full-time jobs. For many years, he had this insane expectation I would leave the office at a very specific time so I could get dinner on the table exactly ninety minutes later. That was increasingly difficult to manage over the years as my job demands increased, driven by my upward progression. The better I performed, the more in demand I became and the more time I needed to be at the office. Getting home at a specific minute every day became harder and harder—and absurd as an expectation, frankly.

At some point, he accepted the day-to-day time demands that came with my success. Eventually, my job took me through several years of international travel to investigate allegations of corruption and bribery of foreign officials around the world. Then, the demands for my time were met with anger when I didn't answer his calls immediately. Usually, he needed something that wasn't important in the grand scheme, like my input on the location of some tool. I retained a catalog memory of where "stuff" was stored, which amazes me considering my ability to dissociate along with the vast number of tools, equipment, and materials—often in duplicate or triplicate—we owned with a full working ranch.

Sometimes, he wouldn't reach me on his first attempt.

"Where are you?" he'd react in a sharp tone once we connected. "I've been trying to call you. I can't find the wrench we were using last weekend on the tractor. Where is it?"

"I'm sorry; I was in a meeting with my boss, and I didn't have my cell phone with me," I'd answer, my heart sinking into my stomach as I braced for more. I could hear him sigh as he built up for his next outburst. I pictured him, angry and standing in the building surrounded by all that unorganized "stuff." Standing in the chaos.

"You answer that phone immediately when I call you! That's why you have it!" The condescension echoed in his voice. "You have that phone so I can reach you anytime, no matter what. As usual, your job is more important than me?!" At this point, he was yelling, and I couldn't hear myself think. "I'm so tired of your job being your priority. It's all you care about!!"

"I'm sorry, Tristan, you know that's not true. I got called into his office on short notice and accidentally left my phone behind. It wasn't intentional."

"That phone better be on you at all times! And when I call, you answer!" he demanded.

"I'm trying, Tristan. I'll do better. I'll try to remember to have my phone with me."

I really did try. But in the late 2000s, having your cell phone attached like another appendage, as it is today, wasn't a thing. While Tristan was angry when he couldn't reach me immediately, on the other side I got questioning looks from colleagues and clients if they saw my cell phone outside of my bag. This worrisome balancing act stressed me out. And again, there was no real reason for his behavior.

His reaction to not being able to reach me immediately wasn't warranted. Nothing he said was true, but it also wasn't worth arguing. He just never accepted the demands of my job—which paid for our lifestyle—and the resulting pressure on me. The compounding effect of his constant and increasingly unreasonable demands pushed me to an unhealthy place.

Not too many years after the Big Bend Open Road Race, I bought a used, white, manual-transmission 2000 Mazda Miata MX-5. Convertible. Every Miata enthusiast who owns a soft-top convertible wants the hardtop, too. The hardtop is much better in the winter to keep the elements out. Plus, it just looks cool and gives the car an entirely different look. But hardtops are difficult to come by on older models. I'm lucky to have one.

I've had the car for more than fifteen years, and it is still today one of my rare, prized possessions. It's nothing fancy—simple, like me. I love the exhilaration of pushing the car through its five speeds. I'd always dreamed of restoring it my way. That never happened until recently, when I began the process.

When Tristan and I divorced, I pretty much walked away. I only wanted my freedom and did what I had to do to get it. That meant walking away from almost every material possession—and what they had symbolized—that had been in my life before I moved to Hong Kong, all of which were in Conifer. The summer before our divorce was final, I visited the house in Conifer while Tristan was in Thailand. I went to get "my stuff," having no idea what that would mean when I arrived. That's when I drove away with just the coffee table and the twelve bankers' boxes in the back of a Suburban. I left my Miata behind.

Thankfully, at the very last minute of negotiating our divorce settlement, someone who knew what the car meant to me told me to get it. I paid Tristan $900 for it. I shouldn't have paid him one cent more than our settlement already dictated, but it was worth it to me, and I probably would have given him more. My Miata is much more than a car to me. I've begun to work on it, which is the realization of a personal dream—doing something for myself that I wanted to do for more than fifteen years—but a dream shelved while I put everyone and everything else first.

The awful reality is that I had no awareness I was so lost behind my wall. I didn't even know it existed until I began to learn about my unhealthy survivorship. Soon after discovering it, I knew my only way forward, to break it down, was to HEAL. So I did.

I came up with the acronym HEAL to describe what healing means to me. To HEAL means to Hope, Evolve, And Love. As we progress in this book, I will share my story about each of these aspects of my healing journey and how I live today as I continue to heal. I'll tell you about my experience with *hope* and staying hopeful. You'll see my *evolution* in two parts. First, through my healing process, including the tools I continue using. Second, you'll see my self-evolution in discovering who I am, which enabled me to deal with hurtful relationships. Finally, I'll share my journey with knowing *love*, embracing it, and holding dear its true meaning.

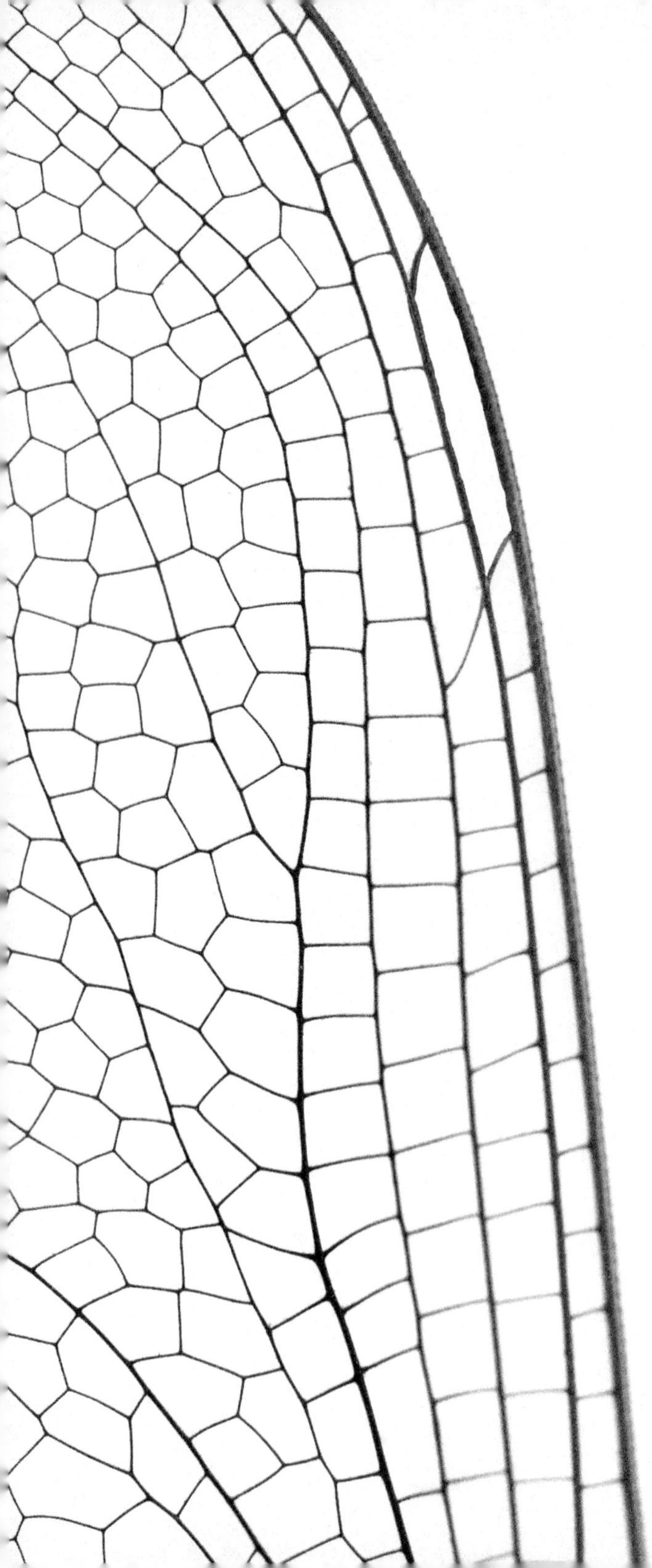

PART II
—
HOPE

Hope is my "H" in HEAL because hope fuels the healing process for us as survivors. We must keep hope at our core, sustaining us as we walk our healing pathway. Hope keeps us going when our journey gets tough.

EVERY ONE OF us who wants to heal must do our own work to get there. No one can do it for us. But the hard part about walking the journey—the part that may throw some of us off the path momentarily, temporarily, or forever—is that along the way, we will likely encounter deeply painful emotions. Many of us will be triggered by remembering events or feelings from our past. Some of us may suffer more trauma while working to heal. Sometimes, we may feel we're going backward from the forward progress we thought we had made.

Those things—what some might call setbacks—can be hope killers. But my experience repeatedly shows that we can move past them.

When I look at other people who have healed or are trying to heal, I see that hope is all around. I've read enough about recovering from the effects of trauma—books based on observation of others' experiences—to know healing is possible, no matter what we may have experienced that tried to rob us of joy and love. As I continue to share my story and people engage with me to share their stories, I hear directly about their similar experiences. I learn of trauma and a life encumbered by unhealthy survivorship as they work to live a healthier life.

I've talked to plenty of women and men who have been sexually abused. These days, I wonder whether this experience is more normal than not. Then there's my colleague who, around my age, began to deal with the trauma of living with a father who he could never please and a survivorship that eventually wrecked his marriage. Or my friend who recognized he was casting his own survivor's trauma and abuse onto his son and then chose to heal before his child suffered more harm. Or a woman I met not too long ago who went from being homeless with four kids, taking desperate actions to survive, to becoming an executive with a Fortune 50 tech company.

And I have my own personal experience with evolution and transformation. Because of the data I've collected, I know it's possible to thrive after surviving trauma.

But what happens when you don't have hope or you lose hope after encountering a hope killer? Can you recover hope once it's lost? If so, how? I've been in this place too.

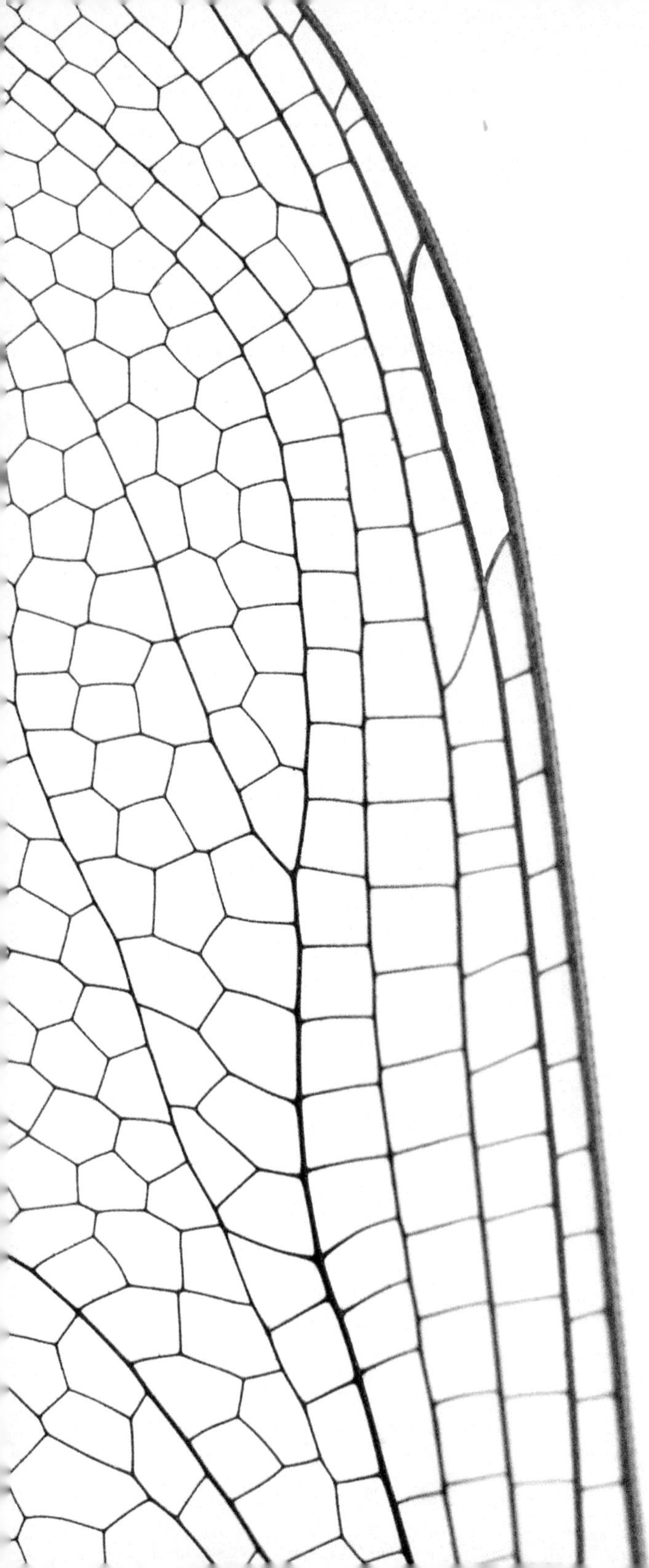

CHAPTER 4

LOSING OPTIMISM

HOPE IS AT the core of who I am. I'm naturally an optimist. In fact, I'm so hopeful that rather than describing myself as a glass-half-full girl, I say I'm a "glass-three-quarters-full girl." Being a natural-born problem-solver means I tend to live with the view that no problem is so insurmountable that it can't be overcome. I believe there's *always* a way forward.

My nature is so optimistic that sometimes I can irritate people, especially if they're more pessimistic or even catastrophic or fatalistic in their thinking or if they're like me—naturally hopeful—but have dealt with repeated trauma and challenges that cause them to waver. In some cases, these people have lost all hope.

Tristan got irritated with my hope. He was a dreamer, full of perseverance and commitment, so I would describe him as a hopeful person too. But he fought a lot of challenges from a very early age. He had setbacks, many of which I lived through with him, and I experienced his anger when he lost hope.

Once, we were installing an underground power line from our house to a barn we were building. We dug the trench about three feet deep, but we hadn't laid the power line, so the trench was completely exposed. It was just wide enough to trap a goat, and that is exactly what happened in one of our many, many chaotic events.

I don't remember exactly the cause, but one of our nanny goats, who may have been pregnant at the time, fell upside down in the trench and became lodged so tightly we could not pull her out. Tristan frantically tried to deal with her escalating suffering, mainly trying to keep the sand out of her nose and mouth while also trying to give her water. Summertime in Texas can bring long periods of no rain, which meant the sandy loam soil was dry like fine beach sand, and it kept caving in on the goat. Even the dirt worked against us that day.

The nanny goat was suspended in the upper half of the trench, her belly spreading out across her sides, trapping her as she fell in. The most logical option to get her out would have been to dig around her. But we could clearly see that the damn dirt—the dry sandy loam—would completely cave in on top of her as we dug, and she consequently would slide down to the bottom of the trench. We would have buried her alive. So, digging around her was not an option.

During the struggle, my optimistic, problem-solving nature kept suggesting ways we could try to dislodge her. Sometimes, my idea was good, so I would scramble to get whatever tools or equipment the task required, and we would try. But we would fail.

Other times, my idea was bad, and Tristan let me know that with that air of contempt.

"That won't work," he snapped, showing me in his voice and facial expression that I should have already known that. I knew he was thinking, *You've been doing this kind of thing for years* (the ranch hand work I'd done so much of by then); *how could you think THAT would work?* He had this saying, "Ninety-eight percent of people in this world are dumbasses." But he considered us to be the two percenters. Still, more times than I care to remember, he made me feel like a 98 percenter, like a dumbass. This was one of those days.

We struggled back and forth like this for a while with the goat, but we were ultimately unsuccessful. We watched her slip away in what must have been an absolutely horrible and frightening experience for her. Hearing the sound of an animal in extreme pain, fighting for its life, followed by the gurgling sound of its last breaths, and then the ensuing deafening quiet, which comes as its life leaves, is traumatic. Ultimately, we needed the backhoe to get her body out of the trench so we could bury her.

Sadness at her loss gripped both of us. But Tristan was utterly grief-stricken, given his devotion to the animals. I don't know everything he felt that day, but I believe he felt guilty, as her caregiver and protector, that he couldn't rescue her. Saving any animal or insect was always a priority for him. He became frantic, especially as death approached, no matter what else was happening.

He was also what I call a "should've, could've, would've" person, second-guessing after the fact what could have been done differently to change the outcome. I find this practice particularly unhelpful, as it just adds to self-blame for whatever happened, thereby inflicting more trauma. This is *wretched trauma*—that which we inflict on ourselves through our inner critic.

My reaction was to try and console him by telling him the truth. "We didn't do anything wrong; it was just an accident. We tried everything we could to save her; it must have been her time to go. Why that way? I don't know…yes, it was a horrible way to die."

"That's so stupid!" he raged. "We should've covered the trench, and that would've saved her life." How we could've covered the trench, I don't know. The width would not have been the problem, but the trench was over one hundred feet long, and we would have needed a barrier strong enough to withstand livestock putting their hooves through it.

"You're always so damn hopeful, and it infuriates me," his tongue spoke, cold and sharp. Rather than accepting that I was trying to console him, he attacked my optimism and hope. He may as well have slapped me across the face or punched me in the gut. His words and facial expression conveyed contempt to me yet again. I was also hurting over the pain of watching the nanny goat die such a horrible death. And now I hurt even more deeply over his shaming of our attempts to save her, which to him were feeble in retrospect.

Situations like this often happened to us, regardless of whether animals were involved. His subtle attacks on my hope got worse as he went through the many years of injuries, surgeries, and recovery. And I understood his frustration. I felt it, too.

"Stop saying that!" he'd say as I tried to encourage him that he would recover fully enough to run again after surgery on his calf muscles, where his orthopedic surgeon—one of the best in Texas—had to read about performing in a textbook because the procedure was so rare. "If I even make it through this surgery being able to walk, you think I'm *ever* going to run like I did before?!" And there was that scornful look again. Now, I can see much more clearly the extent of his emotions, how they impacted him, and why he would attack my optimism and hope. But I didn't understand back then. This crushed me because he struck a significant part of who I am, part of the essence of my being.

I put the emotions of that day spent fighting for our nanny goat's life in a box and placed the box into my wall. But I didn't lose my hopeful nature—even as my wall got thicker and higher.

Until one day when I lost all hope. As I opened my eyes after coming out of my hypnotized state, a two-ton wrecking ball hit me hard. I was immediately confused, bewildered, and shocked by what my mind revealed. With my hands covering my face, some of my first words were a desperate, sobbing exclamation: "I have *no* idea who I am. Everything about my life is a complete lie!"

Suddenly, everything I believed about myself—including my childhood, marriage, and relationship with family and friends—seemed like that lie because the person at the center of it all, me, wasn't who I thought she was. If I wasn't who I thought I was, my life as I felt I had known it must have been a lie—the polish I had worn in the outward expression of my life suddenly chipped and washed away. My hope vanished, too.

How on Earth would I problem-solve through dissecting fifty years of my life? I couldn't even remember most of it because of my dissociative amnesia—which I was about to meet up close and personal. With profound despair, I felt like my core was ripped out of me—both my beliefs about who I was and my hope. And, of course, Tristan's reaction to me that day only made things worse. I'd committed more than thirty years to that man, but he could not meet me with the same commitment in my most desperate time of need. Perhaps he would have reacted differently if I had fur and were upside down in a trench. Another hope killer.

Although I had experienced feelings of loneliness before this happened, I was okay with it—good, in fact. I'd always been a bit of a loner, an independent girl and woman, and I was comfortable being alone in my solitude. Sometimes, I need it to separate from the chaos in my life. But this familiar feeling, satisfying a need, wasn't what I felt then. Instead, I felt, perhaps for the first time, the loneliness that had become part of my existence as I lived behind my wall. *There's no one out there to help me*, my inner critic told me, as despair consumed me. *No one cares about me or about helping me. Not even Tristan. I'm all alone, just as I've always been.*

And because there was no one to help me, there was no one to give me hope. Only *I* could help myself. Which is one of the truths about healing. There is no part of the healing process that anyone can do for you.

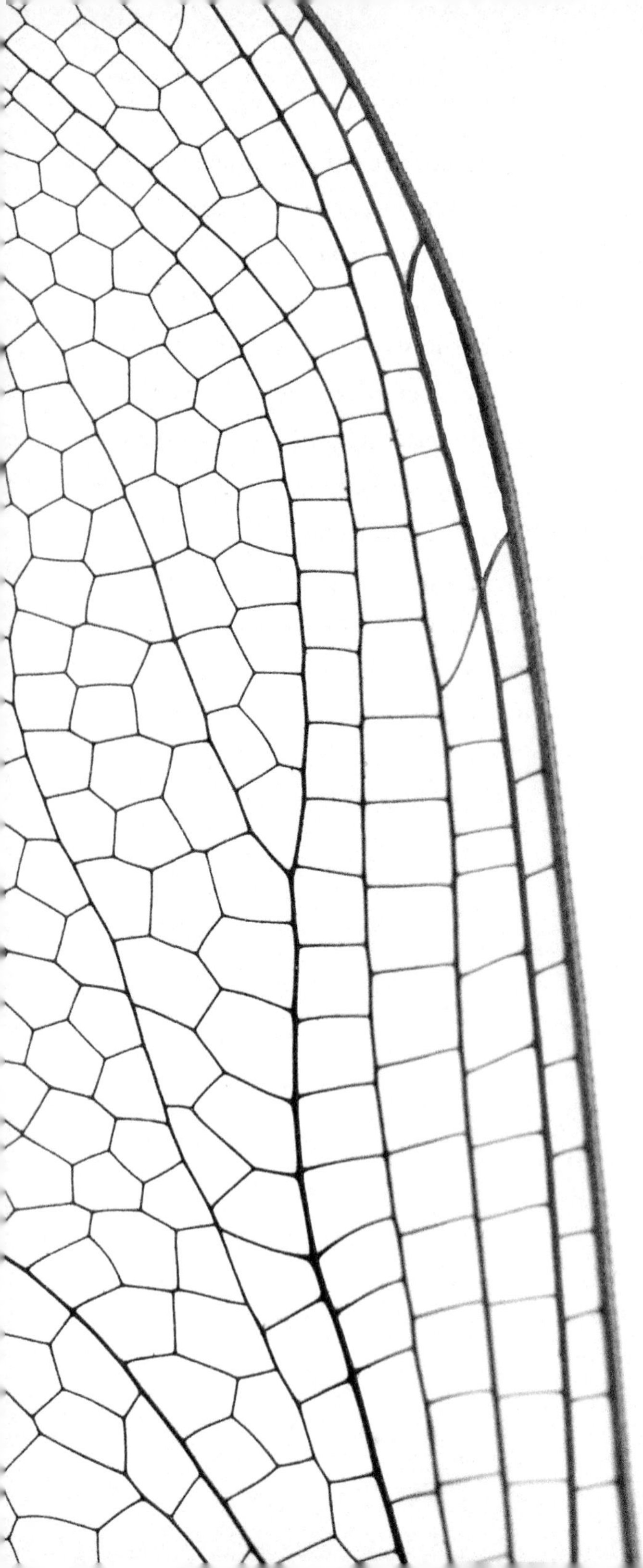

CHAPTER 5

REIGNITING RESOLVE

FOR ME, THAT lesson began with my work to recover my hope. Through my ever-present search to connect with my spirituality, the Universe started to work wonders and help me. I told Sally and Kate about the outcome of my hypnotherapy session despite my fear of revealing this. And they met me with compassion and empathy. Their acceptance and support would become vital in recovering my hope. They saw me as the same person they had always known and loved, not someone who was suddenly different due to my experiences.

Before that night, I'd rarely felt so much care for me. It's not that people didn't care for me, but I don't recall feeling compassion like I sensed that night. That was one of the first real acts of love I experienced through my healing journey and search for love. Though I didn't know what it was then, I began to feel a small fraction of hope.

The following day, because of the words Sally had said to me—"sexual abuse" and "therapy"—I searched the internet for a "child sexual abuse therapist." But I had little hope I would find what I needed. First, I had no idea what I was looking for. I thought back to my years of therapy, which hadn't produced results. Plus, I was in Hong Kong, a place where being open about mental health or a topic like child sexual abuse was taboo.

As I typed my search string, I felt trepidation rooted in so much doubt that anything helpful would come back. But, to my great surprise, two search hits came up immediately. One was a trauma therapist—precisely who I was looking for. The other was surprising because it came out of the blue. Finding a support group in Hong Kong was jaw-droppingly unbelievable to me.

Both connections led to great stories unfolding in my healing pathway. Both profoundly impacted me and my healing right from the beginning. And both helped to reignite my hope that I could get the help Sally told me I needed.

The trauma therapist was Monica Borschel. When I saw Monica's name that morning, I knew I had seen it somewhere. I was relieved to find a therapist advertising as a trauma specialist, including, more specifically, with child sexual abuse (sometimes abbreviated in this book as CSA). The next step would be exploring rapport and whether I could work with her, but that would come in time. For now, I had at least found someone in Hong Kong. *Hope.*

Monica's name nagged at me increasingly intensely for a couple of weeks. It sounded so familiar that I searched my smartphone for her name. And there it was, in my contacts and a text message exchange years before.

Shortly after I moved to Hong Kong, we connected briefly. I was in one of my periods where I knew I needed help emotionally—therapeutic help—but I didn't understand why I needed it. Since I didn't know why, I also didn't know what to work on. We had a few sessions together but then parted ways for one reason or another. Our parting had nothing to do with her. *Maybe she can help me,* I thought. *I liked her.* Within days, I tracked her down; the rest is history, as they say.

The support group hit on my internet search was TALK Hong Kong, an English-language peer-led support group for adult female survivors of sexual abuse, regardless of whether they were abused as a child or an adult. It shocked me to consider this as a viable option because I didn't have a support group in my head as a place to get help. It never occurred to me until I saw it.

If you had asked me then what I knew about support groups, I would only have been able to mention Alcoholics Anonymous (AA), Al-Anon, and Weight Watchers—without offering much else. I wouldn't have associated these groups—not even AA—with survivors or survivorship, nor would I have associated myself as a survivor who would benefit from a group.

I had been through a faith-based weight loss program years before. Looking back, I'm sure that some of my eating habits were fueled by stress in my early days of chaos. By going to that group, I got help to manage what could have become a more significant part of burying myself behind my wall—obesity and its related health issues caused by stress eating.

Seeing TALK sparked my interest and ignited my hope that day. *More hope.*

I vividly recall the first TALK meeting I attended a couple of weeks later. I was, again, terrified the night of that first meeting. This was my first step with strangers—the public—admitting I needed help because I had been sexually abused as a child. It was an outward admission of something I had just been awakened to, and I was only in my early days of slowly creeping toward accepting my reality.

My imposter syndrome played intensely into my experience at that time. That night, I was having an out-of-body experience, which I would get occasionally. That night, I asked myself some incredulous questions: *Why am I here? Really? I'm here at this meeting about this subject. I'm here, but I shouldn't be here, right? No way! This cannot be, can it?*

Only two other people attended that night: the group's founder and another survivor. The founder, Taura Edgar, began the group just a year before, born out of her healing journey. The newness of a group like this in Hong Kong meant that attendance early on was limited. The meeting was casual and informal, with an agenda and some prepared questions to help spur conversation, though we weren't required to say one word if we weren't feeling it.

The group was named "TALK" for a reason. That's because survivors need to talk about what happened to them in a safe environment with people with shared experiences and, therefore, compassion and empathy for one another. Sharing with other survivors about similar traumas helps us know we are not alone. I've said it before, and I'll repeat it: while it sucks to know we have groups like this—because so many of us have suffered abuse—it's comforting to find others who understand and share in our healing.

I felt an instant connection with Taura that night. Maybe because she so eloquently introduced herself as a survivor of a similar experience to mine. But I was also gripped by her description of TALK, including why she founded it. I felt like she had started the group for me. I was there because she was there—as if I was led straight to her (which I now know is exactly what happened). It seemed like she knew I was coming and that I needed her and the experience of working with TALK in other ways besides being a member. After all, TALK would get me talking outside of my tribe.

I left that night with even more hope restored.

Taura and I became good friends. That alone would have been an incredible benefit from the group, in addition to the healing aspects of participating in meetings. But Taura and I found we had a lot more in common. Divine intervention brought us together. Another Universe touch. Today, not only do we have our shared personal experiences with CSA and survivorship, but we also have our shared purpose in life, which is to help others impacted by trauma and abuse, including CSA. For me, this involves teaching and mentoring survivors along their healing journey, whether they are healing from the effects of CSA or other types of abuse and trauma. For Taura, it's about the prevention of CSA in the first place, before it even becomes a thing for a child and wreaks havoc in their life.

We are taking our stories public—out to the general population—to help others. Taura and I began this journey in public together when we had our first truly "public" appearance in Hong Kong as guests on a talk radio show about CSA. We shared how it has impacted us and why awareness and prevention are vital to protecting children. Neither one of us has looked back since. We're both on a mission to bring light to this darkness, and we've found encouragement and support for one another in our missions.

I'm honored to have served on TALK Hong Kong's first Advisory Network (like a board of directors). The company I worked for did a cool pro bono project for TALK, helping to create visualization of data for a report that TALK issued on the prevalence of CSA in Hong Kong. I'm proud of the project and the report itself, but also that my company supported me with something so personal and important.

My internet search and the events within a short number of weeks afterward—beginning trauma therapy and actively participating in TALK—gave me a lot more hope after the ignition point of telling Sally and Kate. But I still wasn't feeling like my usual, hopeful self. I didn't believe my problem could be solved. I'd been smacked upside the head with the reality that I was a survivor who needed help and didn't know who I was. I needed to take one more significant step on my pathway before I would finally get my hope back: I needed *knowledge*.

Monica and Taura, through TALK, would be my keys to getting this crucial knowledge. They introduced me to two books that fed my thirst to understand trauma response and how survivors cope. These books were *The Courage to Heal: A Guide for Women Survivors of Child Sexual Abuse* by Ellen Bass and Laura Davis and Pete Walker's *Complex PTSD: From Surviving to Thriving*.

Taura brought *The Courage to Heal* to every TALK group meeting. She put it on the table but never pressured anyone to pick it up. The Universe touched me again as I flipped through the first few pages at my initial meeting. I didn't want to put it down, and even though she normally wouldn't part with the book, she let me take it home that night.

I ordered my copy immediately because I *really, really* needed to highlight passages that were significant to me and make notes in the margin. I felt urged to do the exercises. That pretty much happens to every healing-related book I read; dog ears, highlights, and notes cover the pages.

Since I couldn't mark Taura's copy of the book, I ordered my own. This may seem like a *so-what. You ordered your own copy*, but at the time, the book wasn't available directly in Hong Kong (something Taura and TALK have since rectified). I ordered it through Amazon, which delivers a lot to Hong

Kong, but some goods, including specific book titles, aren't available there. In some ways, Hong Kong resembles mainland China, including with its censorship. Luckily, this title was available and could be shipped to me.

This book—and the discussions I had with Monica about it—helped me to see more clearly and go more deeply into accepting myself as a survivor of CSA. But those discussions led to another brutal realization: my experience in high school was severe, and I had been traumatized and abused, then, too.

Before understanding CSA, I would describe the events of that night as a "date gone wrong." I never accepted myself as a rape survivor or a survivor of bullying. I never recognized the resulting shame I held. And I never accepted that my friends had betrayed me.

The day I accepted these truths about myself, my hope took a large, strident step backward. This time, however, my hope wasn't lost completely like it had been post-hypnotherapy. This taught me how the healing process goes two steps forward and one step backward.

Commonly metaphoric, but a great metaphor here, healing is like being the proverbial onion and peeling away the layers down to the deepest layer of who you are and why you exist. As you peel, you sting from the burn and intense reality of what you discover. You stumble sometimes, taking steps backward to cope with the burn. Sometimes, it's a *big* step backward, and you must pause to recover before you can move forward again. Even as hard as the backward processing can be, and even if your eyes sting as you cry, you are freeing the emotion that needs to come out. In that way, you are processing and progressing.

When I felt despair after uncovering this layer of my being, Monica recommended another book. Remember, I was looking for knowledge at the time, which she knew was important for my analytical brain. She suggested Pete Walker's book.

Reading *Complex PTSD: Surviving to Thriving* allowed me to start developing some academic or clinical understanding of how we survive and cope with trauma. This helped me profoundly because it gave me terms to assign to my attributes that I could only previously describe conceptually, often with painful and contorted explanations. This book is where I discovered the term *parentectomy*—cutting oneself off from one's parents—which is a typical response to my type of trauma. As I read, I thought, *OMG, this exiling of one's parents happens to so many survivors that someone made up the perfect word for it!* That is, an "ectomy," or *cutting off something trying to kill me.*

I also got my understanding of *dissociative amnesia* from Walker's book. Reading about the condition brought one of my more significant Universe touches because I finally had an explanation for what happened to my memories, but more importantly, why I didn't have memories like others did. I had been in survival mode for a very, very long time!

I could see my inner critic—who I met for the first time as I read Walker's book—so clearly in my thoughts about myself. Perfectionism attacks, self-disgust and toxic shame, guilt, should-ing, and busyholism (the chaos), which were all me. As my understanding of trauma survival developed, I could also see that the damage we do to ourselves through self-criticism and negative self-talk is perhaps some of the worst trauma we survive. We harm ourselves for no other reason than that we are survivors, which is a cruel irony of being a survivor.

"Triggers," which I could only describe previously as events that made me cry for no apparent reason, began making sense. Now I knew why I cried when I saw a dad and daughter, or husband and wife, on TV in a loving interaction. That loving feeling expressed through an embrace or a supportive discussion, at least the way I perceived it, was something I had rarely experienced. My sobbing was an expression of my sadness about that, even though, for years, I didn't know why I was crying. My tears were reactions to triggers—encounters that made me feel (or relive) the pain of my trauma and emotional abuse.

The Universe touched me again, I thought *because now I understand there's a cause for my odd reactions at times.* As I developed my vocabulary to understand myself as a survivor, I also realized that *People out there are trying to give us the tools to heal. And people are healing.* That meant I, too, could HEAL. This BIG Universe touch finally gave me my hope back.

These events I've described to reignite my hope occurred over three months, wherein I was led step-by-step. Looking back, I see so much evidence that my Higher Power led my healing journey during those months. And these events that led to me getting my hope back were foundational to my healing—the essence of who I am returned. I was no longer completely disappearing under the weight of what I'd discovered about myself. Instead, that pain was my fuel to keep moving forward and fighting to heal.

Today, I believe my Higher Power leads me down a divinely created pathway that is my life's purpose. The phenomenon of seeing this in action regularly continues today. And I haven't lost my hope again.

As I walk on my healing journey, hope sustains me. The fuel that drives the feedback loop of my healing, creating a self-perpetuating wheel, is hope. As I work to heal, I make progress, which I can see and rely on to keep me going, even during setbacks. This prompts me to do more work in the area that needs it most at the time. Sometimes, I need to move past the setback. Sometimes, I work on advancing my healing and continuing to overcome or mitigate my unhealthy survivorship. Other times, I'm learning about myself and discovering who I am. And through it all, I'm moving to fulfill my highest and most significant purpose in life—nearing the top of my *second mountain*, as described in David Brooks's book *Second Mountain: The Quest for A Moral Life*.

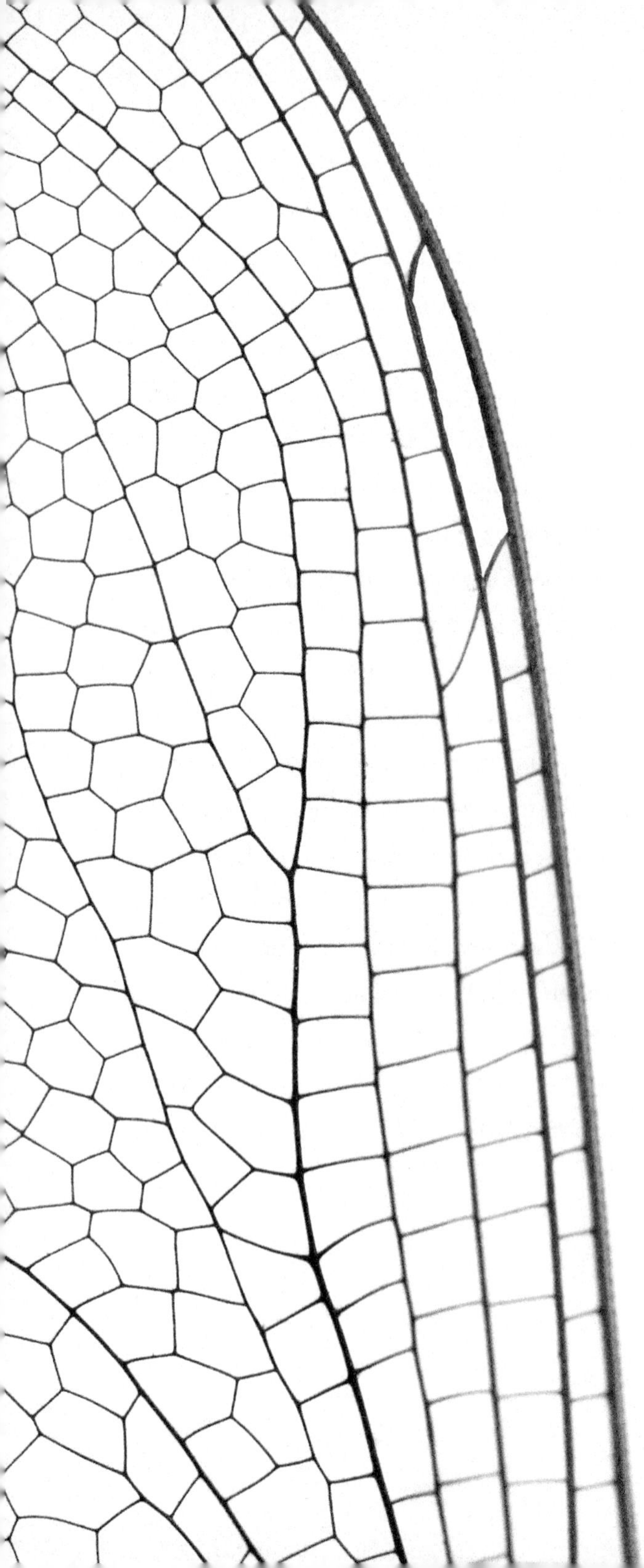

PART III
—
EVOLVE

Evolve is my "E" in HEAL because the healing process for survivors requires us to evolve as human beings. We must evolve both in our healing and as people. The work to evolve is hard and sometimes painful, but the outcome, love, is worth it.

AT THE HEART of connection and socialization are relationships with others. Indeed, my healing journey began with a simple desire to learn why I had difficulty making authentic connections with people. Receiving the connection, satisfaction, and love we seek requires us to engage healthily. As survivors, however, many of us have been hurt by others. In some cases, we've reacted by engaging in unhealthy relationships.

Evolution is an evitable truth for human beings. We evolve as we adapt to our environment and experiences, which has been true since the dawn of humanity. We see this through the ages as human civilization has modernized to the point where we recognize today's technological and social advancements. Our global focus on green transition to offset climate change and our work toward common human rights and social equity are examples. Even events such as the 9/11 terrorist attacks in the US or the global Covid-19 pandemic—and the ensuing impact on the way we travel and work—are clear examples of human evolution.

In my experience, healing has two parts that involve evolution. The first part is the evolution of the healing process, refining how we use various tools to work specifically for us as we recover and become healthier. The second part is self-evolution, including self-discovery of both the favorable and the difficult within us. Evolution enables us to learn and accept both sides of ourselves—who we are and why we react or respond as we do. Both are part of our evolution as survivors.

How did I go from having no idea who I was post-hypnotherapy to my current confidence in who I am and my life's purpose? I evolved. And it all began with that hypnotherapy session.

This is another healing truth I have learned. If we're not ready, we won't heal. Because I wasn't ready before that day, nothing ever clicked in my brain—not even after the remarkable coincidence I had experienced fifteen years earlier when my Aunt Cheeto told her truth. Healing would require me to evolve, but I could only do that when I was truly ready. And I wasn't ready to do the hard work to *really* heal until the day I tried hypnotherapy.

As I take you through my *evolution*, remember the sustaining power of my *hope*.

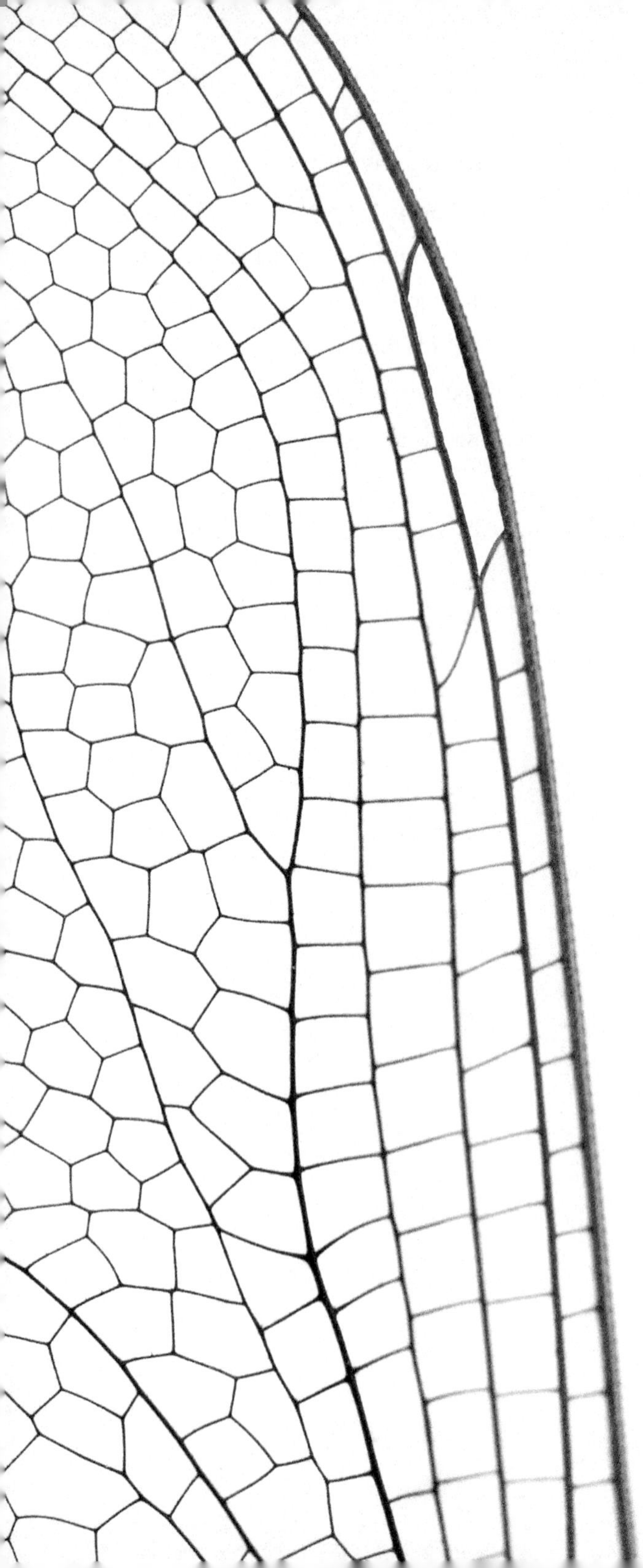

CHAPTER 6

EXPLORING HEALING TOOLS

As I've shared, a series of events up to and including hypnotherapy put me on the pathway of my healing journey. Hypnotherapy then helped me cross the dividing line between the juxtapositions in my life: bringing light to my darkness, truth over family secrets, and a healthy me instead of an unhealthy me. Kate called the hypnotism my "moment of spontaneous combustion." As I look back over my life, however, the mounting pressure on me to heal began much earlier than this. My beginning might have been when I left home for college at the age of seventeen.

In college, though I was in the care of my grandparents and therefore exposed to the danger of my grandfather, the Pacific Ocean literally separated me from my parents and the emotionally unsafe environment I had lived in for years as a kid. Going to college was my first escape and break from that life of Jekyll and Hyde and my parents' ensuing arguments, my dad's incessant teasing, and my mom's attention being focused on everyone except me. Although I can see how leaving home might have been an aided trauma response of *flight*, it was through going to college that I first experienced the importance of separating from a traumatizing environment.

After college, and for more than twenty-five years before my hypnotherapy session, from time to time, I did try, unsuccessfully, to do the work to heal. I engaged with various tools. I tried this. I tried that. All failed, and I remained exactly where I was, stuck, just surviving while trauma and abuse continued to build a wall around me.

Post-hypnotherapy, I had a lot more success because I took control of the healing tools I was already using and made them work for me. I also used new tools. To illustrate, I'm going to tell you about three critical tools and how I evolved in using them to advance my healing. The first two worked together for me. One is my evolution with counselor-led therapy, from couch therapy to trauma therapy. And the other is how my healing has evolved through movement. The third is my ability to deal with triggers.

Counselor-Led Therapy

At various times during our marriage, Tristan and I went to couple's therapy. We went at his request almost every time—if not every time. Although I believe he was trying to keep us together, I always felt like we were there more to change something about me rather than something about us. In fact, for some period, our marriage counselor was also his individual counselor. Of course, she probably advised against this as a general best practice, and I must have agreed to it, but the conflict between her roles was a problem, at least for me.

We were both doing individual counseling, which I believe is imperative if two people in a relationship desire to succeed in their therapy work together. Consider that a relationship lies on a scale where each person is between 0 and 100 percent at fault. But of course, no one is ever 0 percent or 100 percent at fault. Instead, each person shifts around on this scale depending on the situation's circumstances. In this way, both are "at fault," to a certain degree, for whatever is happening. Individual therapy work helps an individual see where they're contributing to the "fault," which is why working on oneself is so vital to the success of a couple's therapy.

Said another way, healing isn't about the *him/her* or the *us* of a relationship. Instead, healing is *only* about each person as an individual. Too often, we analyze the other person and vilify them for what they have done to us. That's a waste of time if we haven't done our work to heal. And once we've done the work, we probably aren't vilifying as we once did.

Although I tried, I couldn't get much help from my therapy during those years. This is when a lot of that uncontrollable sobbing I described earlier occurred. Witnessing the loving relationships between a daughter and her father or a wife and her husband on a TV or movie screen triggered my reaction. The same thing would happen while sitting on the couch in therapy. I never knew why I was there, but I was responding to an innate urge at the core of my being to get help. I went because I knew I needed to be there, but I couldn't tell the therapist why or what issue I needed help with; I didn't know those things back then.

When I look back at those years, the frustrating part is that not one of those therapists—and there were many—did any work to help me excavate the source of the emotions flowing as rivers of tears down my face. We talked about whatever was happening in my life then and sometimes how I felt on the rare occasion when I had the words to express my emotions. But we never looked backward or inward. Instead, I just sat on a couch.

I stayed with some of those therapists for sustained periods, seeing them off and on. I walked out on others within the first ten minutes of our first meeting. I stayed if I felt any connection or rapport. I walked out when I did not. But despite being my advocate for working with the right therapist, I never progressed. In fact, I regressed because my reaction to my life experiences—the chaos and relationships unsupportive of my emotional needs—continued to build my wall higher and higher and thicker and thicker.

Twice during those years, I tried eye movement desensitization and reprocessing (EMDR) therapy. I don't know why the modality never worked for me back then. This makes me wonder, mainly as I evaluate why EMDR later worked for me with my trauma therapist, Monica. I can even do it successfully with her over Zoom! However, switching to the remote method terrified me when I was forced to.

We began working together in person in Hong Kong in the early days of the COVID-19 pandemic when Hong Kong was under strict control measures. In-person sessions at her clinic were limited, but fortunately, she offered me her precious in-person time rather than seeing me through the remote sessions that had already become common. Perhaps she sensed I was ready to heal and knew she could best help me in person.

We worked together weekly in her clinic for four months. After three months, she told me she was moving to California. My heart sank because I knew I was making great progress, including with EMDR. I was terrified that it would stall or end if we were no longer in person. She offered to try remote working on a trial basis before she left, and if it didn't work, she would help me find someone else in Hong Kong to work with. I didn't have any choice other than to trust her.

My trust in Monica meant I knew how EMDR worked for me with her, and I knew how the modality was helping me process my emotions and the negative "I" statements that my inner critic fed me. I wasn't willing to give any of that up. I had already come too far in such a short time. Thankfully, because of the in-person rapport we had established, remote EMDR worked for me.

My journey with EMDR is one of the best examples of how my healing tools evolved. I learned to engage with and set boundaries around therapy modalities so that they would work for me effectively without triggering me and causing me more trauma.

EMDR helps us process emotions associated with our experiences—trauma experiences, in particular. By the way, this was never explained to me by my previous therapists. It's probably good that EMDR administered more traditionally—processing the actual events and associated reactions, emotions, and "I" statements stored in our memories—never worked back then. I wouldn't have considered the potentially triggering effect of the modality, nor did I know I would need to set my boundaries. This time, however, the boundary I set with Monica was not to excavate memories my brain had dissociated from. I decided that *if my brain was trying to protect me, I would let it for as long as needed.*

The way Monica and I engaged with EMDR was to focus on processing what I referred to as my "bucket of X emotion." My emotions were coming to the surface regularly after I entered trauma therapy, making it easy to identify what they were. However, the source of the emotion was tricky and very difficult to find. When the emotion surfaced—guilt or shame—we would identify it and then plan to process it in a few weeks.

In the intervening time, I focused intently on the emotion, and when it came up, I wrote down whatever was happening to me at the time and/or my thoughts around it. In this way, I gathered my "bucket of X emotion." This was a way of excavating the current source of the emotion.

Gathering my bucket of guilt, for example, looked like this. I might think, *Wow! That's an awful dress; why would someone wear that?* as I passed a woman on an escalator. This would be followed quickly by my inner critic hitting me with guilt: *I'm sooo judgmental!!* Or, after eating a cheeseburger, French fries, and milkshake, I'd tell myself, *Yep, zero self-control; that's going to make me fatter than I already am.* I would write down each of these thoughts to fill up my bucket.

When I was ready, we processed each bucket and worked on replacing the negative emotions and "I" statements with more positive words. For example, *I'm sooo judgmental; what gives me the right?* after passing the person on the escalator would be replaced with *I'm not judgmental; I'm just acknowledging that my style is different from that person's style. And my style perfectly reflects who I am, so naturally, I would never choose the same dress.* And yes, I did train my brain to say it that way, focusing on clothing styles rather than on the other individual. Or: *That milkshake was delicious! I'm in great health, and there's nothing wrong with rewarding myself after completing The Twins,* one of the most strenuous hikes in Hong Kong, up and down two steep hills in quick succession. I then told my inner critic, *Besides, it's cheat day! That meal won't move the scale one ounce.* Today, I'm much less inclined to go straight to the negative, and when I do, I'm gentle with myself as I redirect my inner critic to a more positive place.

Even though I've healed much of my past trauma, I continue to work with Monica. I believe I may always be in therapy. Now, I have evolved to where therapy isn't always about working on something associated with my trauma and survivorship. Rather, it's become more about Monica being part of my support team. Sure, I still go through times when I need the trauma therapy modalities to heal an emotion, but not as often nowadays, and I'm much quicker to respond to heal myself on my own. Our brains have incredible muscle memory; processing that took me weeks in the past can sometimes now be done in one session.

Today, I have advanced to use variations of EMDR, like brainspotting. The engagement of visual space in brainspotting is like EMDR, but it's less stimulating, thereby tapping into where trauma is stored in the brain rather than focusing on an event and emotions directly. I use this modality now to expand my thinking, accept myself as a teacher and healing mentor, and minimize my imposter so that imposter doesn't interfere with my ability to share the good news of my gift—my healing journey—with the rest of the world.

My inner critic fought me for some time, causing me to be resistant to the idea that I could help others. Thankfully, I'm past that now. But for a while, I struggled with the question of, *What am I?* as I worked to define myself as a teacher and healing mentor. As a humble person, I rejected the idea that I could be "a healer." It seemed arrogant and boastful to think I could "heal" anyone. Indeed, my inner critic kept asking, *Who do you think you are?* in the snarky, mocking tone I would hear when she got fired up.

Through brainspotting and a little EMDR, I accepted myself for what I was born to be. Based on my own experiences, I am someone who helps others find their path through healing while holding a safe and trusted space where they can talk and walk. I knew I accepted myself as the messenger for this work when I finally said it out loud. "I'm a teacher and healing mentor," I blurted out one evening to a former colleague as we talked about my *second mountain* work, as author David Brooks wrote about. The words *healing mentor* rolled right off my tongue, just like they belonged there. I was startled and took note...with pride.

Movement

After working with EMDR in this way for a few months, my mind began to incorporate the rhythmic aspects of this modality into my physical activity. I enjoy the outdoors, including being in nature, coupled with the dichotomy of an urban environment, as reflected in some neighborhoods of Hong Kong. Where I lived contains a beautiful combination. This creates an urban oasis—a residential part of the city anchored around a golf course where cars are prohibited. Getting around there occurs on foot or by public bus or golf cart. All public spaces are beautified with garden-style landscaping, and many residents have gardens—sometimes arranged in beautiful oriental pots around their property.

Greenery and flowers are abundant year-round. So are the birds. The island has several beaches. My favorite, the "secret" beach, was a short walk through the jungle down a steep incline just below my apartment.

I found the therapeutic benefits of running at the ripe age of thirty-seven. I ran my first half marathon just three months after discovering I could easily take distance. I soon became aware of the mental and emotional processing during my runs. To this day, this is a time when I can work on solving problems—sometimes professionally, but more often personally. At times during my runs, I've prepared my words for a difficult conversation with a colleague or tackled writer's block on a report for a project. Sometimes, I have such great material flowing into my mind that I immediately start writing when I get home. *Drink water. Write frantically before the words are lost. And then shower.* Before you ask, I don't run with music because I prefer the morning sounds of nature waking up. So, I don't have my smartphone to record a voice note.

For thirteen years, during my runs and before I had success working with Monica and EMDR, I worked through many ideas to solve the chaos in my life. Often, these ideas related to whatever construction or repair project Tristan and I were working on at the time. Other times, they involved working out a problem with someone like a contractor or the renter in Combine who destroyed that house, avoiding bankruptcy, or dealing with Tristan. Often, I left my emotions on the pavement rather than burying them.

Yet my wall kept building. I suppose if I hadn't been able to process some of those emotions in real-time and solve the related problem, my wall might have become a fortress that I might never have escaped, no matter how successful my future with Monica was.

I usually take in and remember the scenery when I run, often through five-senses grounding work. *What do I see? What do I smell? What do I taste? What do I hear? What do I feel?* During the months when Monica and I were fully immersed in my EMDR therapy, however, I found that running became an extension of my sessions and much less about self-care. The cadence of following her fingers or a penlight during EMDR seemed to correlate in my brain to the cadence of my stride.

My processing can get very deep when my brain is ready to engage this way. Once, my processing was so deep that I ran a five-mile course, and at the end, I couldn't remember the route I took. I'm pretty sure no five-senses grounding work occurred that day; otherwise, I would have at least remembered that! What I do remember is leaving a lot of emotion—anger, and sadness—on the streets of Hong Kong during that time. A lot of it was associated with our divorce and the trauma of negotiating our separation.

I walk more than run now, trying to preserve a painful knee and aging feet. Even at my slower pace, I can still process. It seems there's a cadence at any pace, which puts me in a state of deep processing.

Movement might not work for everyone. But every one of us can find something that does work. I'll write more about this at the end of this book in the section titled "Tools to Heal."

Dealing with Triggers

As a survivor, triggers are a norm that must be lived with. Triggers cause that back-and-forth progress I've talked about already. Two steps forward, and then something will trigger us to feel like we've stepped backward. Though the backward steps can knock the wind out of us, they bring opportunities to evolve our healing. Often, they help us remember or refine a lesson.

Alright, I'll be honest. Sometimes, these lessons feel like remedial learning. The Universe says, "You haven't quite got it right, so let's do it again." For example, I experienced a lot in my thirty-year marriage related to survivorship that I didn't see and therefore didn't learn from. As a result, after my divorce, I was made to learn some of what the Universe sought to teach me in another, more complicated relationship.

John was a survivor who refused to heal. He lived in alcoholism and chose daily to abandon me for the bottle. Quickly, my kindness in helping him became an expectation he took advantage of, and I could see myself rescuing him, just like I had with Tristan. As I moved toward exiting that relationship, I could see my remedial learning. I joke that it took me thirty years to learn my lessons the first time, which

I didn't quite get. But the second time, it only took me two years—all thanks to the strength of my muscle memory!

All joking aside, dealing with triggers more quickly shows an evolution in my healing. There is no better example of this than what happened to me emotionally as I decided to write this book.

I loved John deeply. There will always be a place for him in my heart because of some amazing things he did for me as my healing progressed. For example, he pushed me to continue my work, particularly concerning my relationship with my parents and taking back my family name, Jones. I didn't want to carry someone else's name after my divorce, but I struggled to accept the Jones name because of the ugly part of our family history. It was John, hearing my resistance and responding with understanding and support, who eventually led me to take back my family name.

"That's a filthy, dirty name," I explained to him as we discussed my intention to give up my married surname as soon as my divorce was final. I wanted the freedom that releasing my married surname reflected. "I'll *never* carry that name again." I was emphatic in my statement.

"Jones is a fine Welsh name. There have been really good people throughout history who carried that name proudly. One person's bad actions don't wipe away all the good in this world that has ever been done by people carrying that name," he pleaded.

"Well, it's not going to be *that* name. I can pretty much adopt any name I want! Who says it has to be a name that is attached to me in some way? Maybe I'll take your name!"

And then John took me through a process to give me another name. We used this privately between the two of us: my given first name, the middle name of his grandfather (whom he adored), and his last name (which he was proud of). He was kind and understanding as we talked it through. And he was utterly selfless in giving up something to which he had attached fond memories to help me work through my pain. He also didn't create an unfounded assumption in his mind that I was insinuating something about our future marriage—that I wasn't. And it worked. The conversation was just about a name and my pain associated with it. He understood perfectly.

Today, I proudly wear the Jones name, signifying how far I've come in my healing journey. And yes, this is one of the twelve times in my life that I've learned the lesson: *never say never.*

I also feel deep compassion and empathy for John as he suffers terribly under the weight of his burden. What he does to himself—extreme dependency on alcohol—impacted me negatively, such that our reactions to each other at times were emotionally unsafe for both of us. As we entered the beginning of the end of our relationship, his provocations caused me to react in anger. Over time, he became more and more defensive, ultimately calling me by vile and profane names. I had progressed enough in my healing by then to exit the relationship, despite what my heart felt. Our relationship no longer served my highest and greatest good, and my head knew what was best for me.

Along with this decision came a significant amount of grief, deep sadness, and anger. The sadness was emotionally and physically draining, and of course, it needed to be processed. The anger also had to go because I had learned it was an emotion I didn't want festering inside of me.

Anger is toxic to the body, emotionally and physically, but its worst effect is closing our hearts. We cannot engage in authentic, loving relationships when our hearts are closed. If anger lives in us, we cannot give or receive love. Hate in our hearts has the same effect, though its impact may be more long-term or permanent.

So, Monica and I worked on the grief. Through our many conversations, I accepted that grief is a natural response to a loved one dying, which is essentially what happened to me, even though he was still alive. I mourned the loss of the person whom I knew he was when not inside of a bottle and whom I saw briefly before his unhealthy survivorship consumed him. (To be clear, his alcoholism was there all along, but I ignored the early, subtle—and not-so-subtle—warning signs, even as he tried to hide the extent of his problem.) I gave myself grace and allowed my sadness to pour out. I silenced my inner critic—*you're such a crybaby, and you're so weak*—just because my damn tears were flowing again. *No, I'm just grieving, and for good reason,* I thought to myself. This time, I knew exactly why my tears were flowing.

For the reason I mentioned earlier, the anger also had to go. My anger was two-part. First, admittedly, I was angry with the Universe for giving me John. He had helped me so much with aspects of my healing in the early days of our relationship. This caused me to fall deeply in love, but then he was taken away from me. Of course, I knew that his choices were what caused me to end the relationship, but still, I was angry.

I was also angry with John for not healing. That, too, I knew was because he was a survivor who most likely wasn't ready to heal for one reason or another. It wasn't his time, and I accepted that his time to heal may not come in this lifetime. His soul may be here to suffer.

Still, I was angry because I felt I was the living testament to what healing could do to bring joy and reciprocal, healthy love to a relationship. I wondered, *Why on Earth are you with me if you're not going to do the damn work to heal?! Why would you choose me? Why would the Universe put you with me?* I had no answers to these questions.

As time moved on, I processed my *why* questions. Since I believed the Universe was guiding me on my life's path, how could I be angry about the path before me? And what right did I have to be angry with someone who was so ill? I knew I was angry with the situation more than anything else. But I would be damned if I was going to allow anger to get in the way of my progress to understand love. Eventually, Monica and I turned to EMDR, and I was finally able to let go of my anger. Or so I thought.

No sooner had my sadness all but dissipated and my anger released when my beloved Aunt Cheeto died unexpectedly. My grief was triggered again. Here came the sadness and anger all over again. My emotions made sense about my aunt, but suddenly, all those same feelings came back over John! Why, when I thought I had already processed them?! I realized my emotions toward him were triggered by her death, but I was so surprised, shocked, exasperated! And frustrated... Suddenly, I felt like my two steps forward had regressed by three steps backward.

My aunt's death deeply saddened me because I don't think she ever had the chance to heal. Trauma and abuse began for her at an early age, resulting in her emotional, mental, and physical suffering. Altogether, this made me deeply sad for her.

I don't have enough memories to say I deeply know most of the people from my past, particularly from my early years, unless I've had the good fortune to reclaim a relationship as I've healed. Couple that with growing up overseas, and I only had limited time in the summer to spend with my aunt. So I didn't deeply know her. But I do remember emotions about her—the way she made me feel—and, of course, my ultimate study of trauma and survivorship later shaped my view of her.

Despite her suffering, she was a fun-loving, outgoing caregiver with the gift of gab who could make you feel like the only center of her world. I can see now her fish lips as she puckered in the way only she could to give me a funny kiss. Sometimes, her eyes were intentionally crossed when mine met hers as she landed my kiss. And sometimes, she made a funny sucking sound as our noses touched. We both would burst out in laughter. And I can still hear her saying "Bethie" with a tone that only her sweet voice could beckon me.

My aunt lived almost her entire life within a fifteen- or twenty-mile radius of where she and my dad grew up in Van, a small town in East Texas. Whereas my dad left the area as soon as possible, my aunt married someone from Van right out of high school, and they never left the area. Their parents had also lived in Van for many years, as did much of the extended family on my dad's side. You could say, Van, Texas, and the immediate area is where the Jones family is from. Many family members still call it home. Not me, though. I'm that citizen of the world.

Van and my aunt's home became a home base during the summers when my family would visit from wherever we were living overseas. Eventually, my parents bought a house there, and we spent even more time in the town during the summer. Despite my dissociative amnesia, some of my happiest memories are from summers in Van and fun-filled time spent with my Aunt Cheeto, Jeannine, Jeannette, and Deanne. I always felt accepted, loved, and safe with them.

My aunt taught me some of life's most essential skills and lessons. I grew up living with people in my home who enhanced our life. The local people in any city I lived in internationally worked in the homes of expatriates as domestic workers. This is an everyday occurrence, not an extravagance, and a common way for the local people in many underdeveloped nations to earn their living. So, as a kid, I never learned how to do routine home maintenance tasks like cooking, housecleaning, and laundry. But my aunt taught me some of these things during the summers because contributing in that way was part of living in her home. Chores must be done, and everyone helped. She was always patient and joked when I didn't get things quite right.

"Sweet Jesus! What on Earth is this? What happened!?" I heard my aunt exclaim one day.

My cousins and I watched soap operas as we waited for the sun to get just right before heading out to the backyard for our Crisco tanning by the swimming pool. We were all intermittently tending to the chores, often distracted by those crucial scenes in the soaps we didn't dare to miss. I was on laundry duty.

"What is this gunk all over these clothes? Oh my, it's all over the inside of the dryer, too!" Her voice was excited, somewhere between laughing and exasperation, as she removed a load from the dryer. She would often bring me the next load to fold, gently reminding me about the timely progression of laundry to completion.

As I heard her say "gunk," I closed my eyes in disbelief. I knew the critical step I had forgotten. "Oh..." I replied sheepishly as I rushed to the laundry area. "I guess I forgot to check pockets like you showed me...."

As she removed the last of the clothing, a tube of lipstick sat at the bottom of the dryer. The tube was empty...because its contents were all over the clothes and the inside of the dryer.

"Bethie, who'd you kill?!" she bellowed with laughter, referring to the red gunk that was everywhere. "We're gonna have a doozy of a time cleaning up this mess!"

She wasn't talking about "we" at all. She patiently watched over me as I cleaned up my mess. Her eagle-eye watched vigilantly. But her love for me did not waver.

My aunt also taught me how to drive during the summers between my sophomore and senior years of high school. This allowed me to get my driver's license before I started college. Just as we'd had domestic workers in our home, we'd also had drivers in every city we resided in, and they took us *everywhere*! I never drove during the school year in those cities, only in the summertime under my aunt's tutelage back in Van.

She taught me and my cousins to drive in a 1972 Buick LeSabre, which was enormous to navigate on the residential streets of that small town. We called it the "Green Olive," though the shade resembled mushed peas. It was the ugliest car I had ever, maybe have ever, seen. But so much joy was found in that car.

"Bethie, that's a stop sign coming up here!" she'd caution excitedly, grabbing the door handle next to her and searching for her passenger-side footbreak. Approaching too fast was sometimes a thing for me. Or she'd say, "Bethie, honey, yellow means slow down, not speed up!" "Heavenly Father, thank you for your hands on the wheel!" was a favorite prayer of hers when I was in the driver's seat.

As a side note, do you think I might have been a little confused about who I was based on the different names I'd been called throughout my life?! On any given day, I might ask, *Am I Elizabeth, Beth, Bethie (or Beffie), or Beth Ann(e)?!* I'd seen and heard them all, though each person seemed to have their own specific variation for me. Still today, I sometimes laugh and wonder, *Did all these names contribute to my imposter syndrome and not knowing who I really was?!*

My aunt also taught me about boys, including how babies are made. She helped me learn about appropriate and healthy relationships through dating. Whereas boys and sex were noexistent topics with my parents, these were open topics with my aunt. My cousins had all engaged in longer-term relationships with boys in high school; some may have begun earlier. Jeannine had married her high school sweetheart. Deanne had lost her high school sweetheart at an early age to a terminal illness before they could marry. My aunt always guided and supported them along the way and did the same for me.

The first boy with whom I had an appropriate and healthy relationship, maybe my first love, was in Van. That connection grew under my aunt's guidance and positive encouragement. But the high school summer romance ended when I went back to Jakarta at the end of the summer. Leaving was the first time I felt true heartbreak. I've experienced it several times since, but that was the defining relationship where I felt my heart shatter for the first time.

During these years, she hung out with us teenagers and was involved in our activities. When the boyfriends visited in the evenings, she was ever-present, certainly chaperoning us and always completely engaged rather than in the shadows. If we were watching a movie, she was right there in her chair beside us. If we played a game or dominoes, she always took her turn. If we swam, she sat by the pool and cheered on whatever water stunt we performed.

As I got older, I thought about how her time with us during my high school summers seemed weird because she was an adult. Now I realize she was probably vicariously living out her childhood and teenage years through her daughters, their friends, and me. She may have been living out a childhood robbed by her father.

My aunt's suffering and the cause of it were not topics discussed. Her pain was so intertwined with—perhaps even at the heart of—secrets held tightly by our family for so long. For years, my family, especially my grandmother and dad, rejected what she had suffered. Her truth lay buried until that day Aunt Cheeto told her truth to her daughters.

What I remember most about the manifestation of her suffering was chronic pain throughout her life. The book *The Body Keeps the Score, Brain, Mind and Body in the Healing of Trauma* by Besser van der Kolk, MD, can help explain what I think was happening to her. Because she never had the opportunity to heal and deal with her unhealthy survivorship, it lived inside of her, manifesting in pain. She took a lot of pain medication. Perhaps this also allowed her to dull her emotions—escaping the experiences she couldn't reconcile.

I was sad when she died because she went to her heaven before I could tell her how impactful her life had been on mine. I've only realized this recently while walking the most intentional and focused part of my healing pathway. We experienced similar trauma inflicted on us by the same abuser. As

I've worked to evolve my healing and understanding of myself as a survivor, I can see the parallels between our lives—both encumbered by unhealthy survivorship. I can also see the positive impact she had on me despite her pain and suffering.

I felt anger over my aunt's death. I was angry for all the same reasons her death saddened me. I was angry at her abuser—my abuser—for sending both of us down the path of suffering. This all seemed so unfair when she died.

Because I felt sadness and anger after my aunt died, those same feelings toward John were triggered again. Again, I felt deep sorrow for him because I realized most likely he, too, would never heal. Again, I felt deep sadness for myself and the love I had lost. And again, I felt deep sadness for us and the loss of what could have been. Again, I was angry at John because he wouldn't do the work to heal. And I was furious at the situation we were in. We wanted to love each other and share our lives, but we were kept apart because of his inability to heal and my expectation that he must. I was unwilling to step so far backward in my healing—into a life of more suffering with someone so afflicted by unhealthy survivorship. I was also angry at myself because I had so much damn hope, too much sometimes, and I simply couldn't let go of what I knew would never be. I knew I was my own worst enemy to move on past him, and this fueled my anger.

So, how did I deal with my emotions over my aunt's death? I went back to a healing tool Monica had helped me develop, which I had used a couple of years earlier during my divorce process. This time, I adapted the tool for my new healing need, pouring out my emotions after my aunt's death. I originally referred to this tool as my "bodysuit," now adapted and evolved into an amphora, an ancient Greek vase.

Monica and I created my bodysuit as a visual image to help me process my heart-constraining emotions toward Tristan. I held a lot of anger toward him and the situation we were in, anger I needed to process out of me. Again, I didn't want those emotions festering and perpetuating my unhealthy survivorship. And I didn't want it to come out at him because angry outbursts wouldn't help us. He didn't deserve my anger.

My head-to-toe bodysuit was made of breathable mesh created from high-tensile threads, which glistened brightly in the sunlight. The mesh felt like silk against my skin and regulated my body temperature, as silk does, and it was painted in bright, vibrant colors. Imagine the colors you might see if you were in Ireland, standing in a lush field of green grass and shamrock, watching the sky set ablaze in color as the sun sets over the deep blue waters of the Atlantic Ocean. Or imagine the colors of a rainbow exploding into a million pieces like Skittles dropping to Earth. The colors were happy, and I felt cozy comfort when I thought about my bodysuit surrounding me. Perhaps I may have even felt joy momentarily when I thought about the beauty of my bodysuit enveloping me.

Whenever I had a message to convey to Tristan, I pushed it out of me through the sieve created by the mesh fabric of my bodysuit. The sieve dissolved the anger before it got out, only allowing peaceful messages to escape from me and go toward him. My messages were delivered on the wings of a white dove.

Of course, my bodysuit was imaginary, existing only in my mind. But this very powerful imagery worked for me. Every time I had a conversation with Tristan, I put on my bodysuit in my mind as if I were putting on my battle armor. The longer I prepared mentally, the better the imagery worked. For the most part, it never failed me after the day I created it.

My bodysuit worked because each message I delivered came out softer than it might otherwise have. This didn't make me emotionless as I had been in our marriage, but the explosive anger I experienced post-hypnotherapy was softening over time. I used my bodysuit a lot as our divorce progressed. As a result, our discussions were productive rather than destructive, focusing on what we each needed in the separation.

One day in therapy after my aunt died, Monica asked me to find a bowl to pour my emotions of sadness and anger into. She was talking about an imaginary bowl, but I understood what she asked me to do. Immediately after her request, my mind created an amphora replica of my bodysuit! I was suddenly standing over a giant vase. It was terracotta but covered with the same vibrant, multi-colored, silken, high-tensile thread that my bodysuit had been made of. It even had the perforation necessary to allow my emotions to dissipate as they flowed out of me and into the vessel. When I saw it in my mind's eye, I was joyful, surprised, agreeable, and understanding simultaneously. The Universe touched me again.

Afterward, I shed tears of sadness and anger into my amphora for days. And it worked just as my mind had intended—again, just like my bodysuit worked during my divorce. This time, the pain of my sadness and anger over my aunt's death and John's inability to heal flowed like a river into and out of my amphora. My tears flowed and flowed.

Until one day, they finally stopped. Another healing evolution was complete.

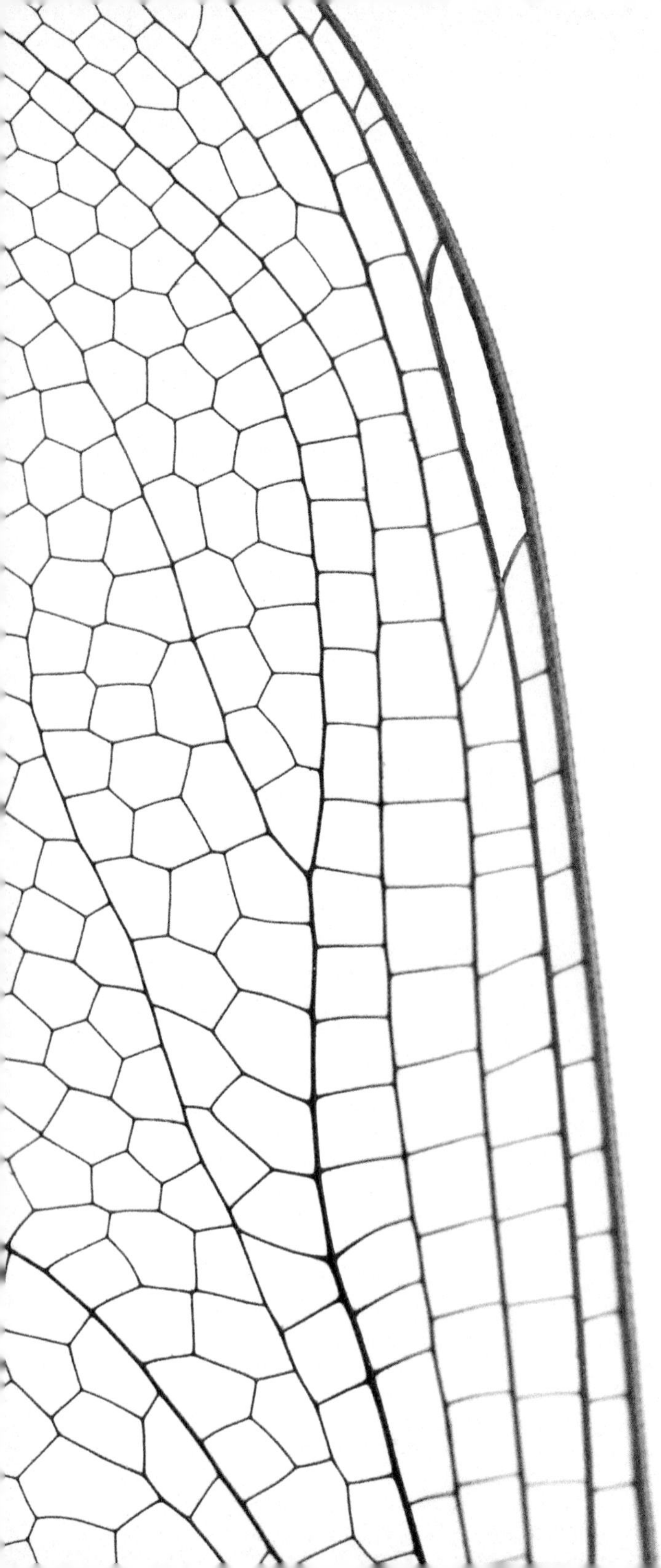

CHAPTER 7

ENGAGING IN SELF-DISCOVERY

I TOUCHED ON this previously, but it's a critical aspect of our healing ability, so I'll say it again. I believe much of the reason we're not able to heal as survivors is that we spend too much time looking at what others did to us. We analyze the other person—our abuser—often vilifying them. In many cases, we live as the victim, stuck in the past.

In my experience, focusing on the behavior of an unhealthy person is a waste of time for at least two reasons. First, barring time with a therapist, friend, or someone else on our support team, when we do this, we're only talking to ourselves in our head. This behavior can trigger and perpetuate the trauma associated with the person. Because we're stuck in our heads and only talking to ourselves, we're not progressing our healing. Instead, how we feel about the other person—usually not good—remains within us. Our thoughts become part of a perpetuating loop of reliving the trauma of our interactions.

Second, their behavior may very well result from their survivorship. This has been my experience with all the significant relationships within which I have been hurt. We cannot do the healing work for someone else. Even if we're in communication and can talk about why they hurt us, they will likely resist, not hearing what we have to say. They won't receive, and they won't heal. Even if they're ready to address their behavior and advance their healing, we may not be the right person to deliver the healing message.

Instead, our best use of time and energy is to focus on ourselves, doing the crucial work to understand who we are. This includes understanding how being both a victim and a survivor has impacted how we live. For me, this meant acknowledging how I'd been trapped behind my massive wall.

As you've probably gathered by now, spending so much time deep in learning about myself has been one of the most powerful aspects of my self-evolution and healing. My work has allowed me to free myself from the bondage of survivorship because I understand why I behave as I do, and I can adjust and evolve where necessary to be healthy. And the healthier me has a heart open to love.

One of the most terrifying things about coming into conscious awareness post-hypnotherapy was the realization that my life as I knew it was shattered. As I've shared, I felt like my entire life was a lie—perhaps one I perpetuated—and I had no idea who I was. In this sobering and life-altering realization, I hit the inside of my wall hard. I had to ask myself: *Why did the wall exist in the first place? And what can I do about it?*

Even in the shock and fear of my realization, somehow, I knew I had a choice. I knew I could remain trapped and crawl even deeper behind my wall, nestled there comfortably like a hermit, perhaps for the rest of my life. Had I made that choice, I would have remained alone and lonely, and I would have given up on joy and love. Or I could choose to face my new reality head-on and deal with it. As the days passed, my choice became clear.

My early healing work was focused almost entirely on myself. This is where I met and got to know my survivorship. As I studied the impact of trauma and the different ways in which we cope, I discovered how my survivorship had manifested in my life. Every single coping mechanism came back to me and my behavior—including my conscious and subconscious decisions. So, to heal, I had to learn about who I was so I could make better choices.

I Learned to Manage My Imposter Syndrome and Quiet My Inner Critic

Imposter syndrome and a loud inner critic plagued me for years. I discovered the depth of my imposter syndrome and the loudness of my inner critic gradually as I healed, and I worked diligently to learn how to manage them.

My inner critic is that wretched abuser, delivering self-inflicted suffering and pain. The ridiculous tales I've told and believed about myself aren't true. They are repressive exaggerations at best and lies at worst. But get a survivor to realize that this critic's assessment is dishonest or disillusioned?... Good luck!

I had heard a lot about imposter syndrome before I began to read about survivorship. However, I had never realized my inability to see myself as others saw me was imposter syndrome. I didn't see the wonderful person I was—the one who my family and friends described me as. I had always gotten positive comments and notes of encouragement, but previously, I struggled to acknowledge that the person they were talking about was me. I also didn't see the bravery others saw in me until I did my work to heal.

Although I was a senior executive—with colleagues and clients who looked to me for guidance in what we referred to as "bet-the-company" crises—I did not see myself as this person. I was good at what I did and honed my skills over time to become an expert, but I still didn't see myself as that person. I had difficulty identifying—verbalizing—even the factual positive attributes about myself, such as saying *I'm an expert in anti-corruption compliance.* I struggled to accept that the expert words coming out of my mouth were my own. I couldn't reconcile that this was part of who I was. I was successful by traditional measures of title and compensation and respected by my colleagues and clients, yet my imposter syndrome persisted in my mind.

It separated me in half. In one out-of-body experience, I could stand in the middle and see two separate people on either side. *You* (on the left) *and you* (on the right) *are the same person?! How can that be? You're just a slight little girl grown up to be plain and unimpressive, not that successful, accomplished business executive.*

To me, I'm just an ordinary person, no better than anyone, and that's who I saw on one side of me. But that wasn't accurate. I have no ego or ideation of self-importance in saying this now, but I was good. Very good, and I got positive results and outcomes for my clients' most complex problems. My skills and expertise were accumulated through hard work over many years. My colleagues and clients knew it. That's why I got hired. That's who stood on the other side of me.

For years, the focus of my inner critic was my appearance. I became a woman late in my adolescence. I was a scrawny girl through eighth grade when all the girls around me seemed to have transformed into women years before. I had braces and thick glasses to boot. My time to fully mature as a woman finally came toward the end of high school. Before then, I felt small, inadequate, and ugly. Those feelings emanated from the girl who was first abused and made to feel inadequate and worthless.

In college, I discovered American fast food. Fast food wasn't a regular thing where I grew up. I remember when the first McDonald's opened in Singapore. We were living in Balikpapan, and my orthodontist was in Singapore, which meant a monthly trip to the island state for my check-ups. McDonald's was such a treat that our luggage allotment on the return flight included an ice chest full of frozen cheeseburgers and Big Macs. Even during high school in Jakarta, where fast food joints were beginning to emerge, my family rarely ate that kind of food. But with easy access to McDonald's, Taco Bell, pizza delivery, and the local Chinese buffet (which wasn't Chinese at all) in Commerce, Texas, I packed on more than a few pounds in college. My beer and liquor consumption didn't help.

By my mid-twenties, when I looked in the mirror, I saw someone who was overweight, sometimes just fat, and unattractive. That's how I saw myself clothed. For many years, I avoided seeing myself naked in a mirror as much as I could. I'm better with mirrors today, but I've still never ogled myself!

For years, it seemed like I vowed daily to get my weight under control.

"You failed," the scale would say each morning.

And then that nasty voice in my head would show up again and again. Sometimes, my reaction to being "too fat" swung to the other extreme of not eating.

"Too skinny." "Too fat." "Too ugly."

Although he never used his words directly with me, I felt the same "too fat, not beautiful enough," chiding from Tristan through his actions or inactions. Over time, I learned to manage my criticism of my weight and appearance, understanding that how I see myself reflects how other people treat me. Damaged goods aren't seen as beautiful. Even though people may damage us, we don't need to adopt the self-inflicted stigma of being *damaged goods*.

Today, I'm much better at seeing the beautiful person I am, inside and out. I'm not as hard on myself. When my weight fluctuates, as it does for many of us as we live and age (haywire hormones as a woman!), I offer myself more grace. Sometimes, I'm just enjoying the holidays with family and friends or getting through a busy or challenging time wherein managing my weight is not—and should not be—my priority. I know I'll eventually get back to taking better care of myself.

For a time, my inner critic told me I'd made two "mistakes" in my relationships with Tristan and John. I later learned to accept that these weren't "mistakes" at all. But until I could become grateful for what I'd learned in each relationship— giving myself grace for being in the relationships in the first place—they, too, were fodder for my inner critic. I questioned my ability to pick a suitable mate, instead focusing on how I'd repeated the same pattern over again. *How stupid am I?* my inner critic began.

I also criticized my artistic ability in still-life and portrait painting, deflecting from what I was good at and loved, which was abstract and mixed-media art. *Tristan was right; you're really not that good of an artist and couldn't have made a living at it, just like he said.*

Even my self-worth came under attack at one point when I had debilitating thoughts about whether I was a lovable person—and a person who deserved to be loved.

Why would anyone love me? Even my parents and Tristan don't love me, so why would anyone else? This question was a gut-wrencher and represented perhaps the hardest I'd been on myself.

Damaged goods...how can damaged goods ever be lovable?

Today, I know those thoughts were nothing more than my imposter syndrome and inner critic attacking me. I was attacking myself.

Both my imposter syndrome and inner critic fed my inability to give my trauma the credit it deserved by calling it what it was. I used to say—seriously, no joke here—that being sexually abused as a child was "just" being "touched inappropriately." And I thought the date rape and bullying in high school were "my fault" and that "I deserved to be ridiculed" because I hadn't known how to satisfy my perpetrator. I even questioned whether these things happened to me at all or if my mind made them up.

For me, this denial of my reality was one of the worst manifestations of my imposter syndrome and inner critic. And as a survivor, that's the cruelest form of trauma: that self-inflicted kind.

Through reading about avoidance or denial of reality as a coping mechanism and engaging in much therapy with

Monica, I overcame this. I'm now very sure about what happened to me, and I'm very sure I did not invite or deserve any of it. I'm also sure that responsibility for these events lies entirely with my perpetrators.

My fiercest bout of imposter syndrome and hardest criticism of myself, however, came recently.

Who am I to think I can help others heal?
Who am I to write this book?
Who am I to think I have anything of value to share with other survivors?
Who am I to think I can teach others about healing?

To know me as Scorpio Rising, born to help us heal, is to know the answer. I'll tell you more in the conclusion of this book, "Helping Us Heal."

When my mind gets going in an unhealthy way, I talk to myself a lot, trying to reason with what I know are ridiculous accusations and attacks on myself. Sometimes, I get downright mad about these crazy thoughts. However, the most effective way I've found to manage this affliction is through positive "I" statements.

When I first started using these, they felt weird and fake to me. But I kept at them, with Monica's persistent encouragement and what seemed like a million Post-it notes taped over my bathroom. Eventually, one day, I looked at myself in the mirror and said out loud, "I am beautiful, inside and out."

Today, the Post-it notes are gone, replaced with phrases that I use as my passwords. These positive "I" statements remind me that: "I am a warrior," "remember who the f@$&

you are," "I have courage to HEAL," and "self-love, first." This has been a powerful healing tool for me because every time I sign into my computer or an app, I'm reminded about the work I have done and am doing to manage my imposter syndrome and quiet my inner critic. I'm reminded of my value and the unique gift I am to this world.

I Opened My Eyes to My Vulnerabilities

I know I tend to be an extreme caregiver. It was so extreme that I had no boundaries on the extent of my caregiving pre-hypnotherapy. I rescued people and was taken advantage of easily.

As a caregiver, most of the decisions I made for many years were for other people and animals, based on their needs and trying to keep them happy. Every waking minute of each day was focused on caregiving for some other being.

In the end, my caregiving became extreme enough to agitate Tristan. One day, he struggled with a zipper on his vest or coat. As I usually did, after only a few seconds of watching him struggle, I pushed him away and took over to fix the problem for him. That day, I brushed his hands aside and grabbed the zipper myself.

"I can do it!" he snapped back in frustration. "Just let me struggle."

I realized that day I was my own worst enemy. Even though my extreme caregiving took so much out of me, I wasn't allowing him to take care of himself. Although

I suddenly recognized my personality trait in that moment, I didn't see my associated vulnerability.

My remedial learning through John, where the pattern began to repeat itself, would teach me. He became the conduit through which I would perpetuate and then see—*really* see—my vulnerability.

I owed John absolutely nothing, yet I began to care for him in ways I should not have. While he pushed back on me initially, he needed a lot of help, which I could give him. So I over-gave. Eventually, he took.

Whereas my caregiving in my marriage grew slowly, with John, I knew what I was doing from the beginning. This time, I expected that his need for my help would end and that he wouldn't take me for granted. He quit his job a few weeks before I returned from Hong Kong. When I returned, we moved in together. I expected he would get another job to do his part to pay our bills. And because he knew about the financial demands Tristan had made of me when we divorced, I expected John wouldn't do anything remotely similar.

He met neither of my expectations.

One day, about five months before we separated for good, we argued about separating. I wanted him to move out; he resisted with everything he had.

"I'm so tired of you and your behavior, John. So tired of you living at the bottom of a bottle. I want you out! Today!!" I demanded. "You've hurt me for the last time!"

In some odd attempt to threaten me or maybe to hurt me, he mocked, "You owe me $5,000 to make me go away."

John was not joking and meant what he said. He was ridiculing me for the decisions I'd made to separate financially from Tristan. And John's acceptance of my help had become an expectation. He may as well have thrown cold water in my face.

Ironically, at the beginning of our relationship, John supported me wholeheartedly as I negotiated my divorce settlement. The financial aspects of my separation from Tristan were the most difficult to navigate, and in the end, I bought my freedom. John understood my need to end the divorce process. He counseled me as I weighed my options. And even though I gave away more than I should have, he encouraged me to do what I thought was best for my needs so I could finally be done and heal my emotions. The emotional toll on me wasn't worth the money Tristan and I were fighting over, and completing our divorce was paramount to my healing. John understood this.

When John later made his financial demand, I was healthy enough to see what he was doing, and I felt angry and betrayed. That day marked my realization that neither of my expectations—that his extreme needs would end or that he wouldn't take me for granted—would be met unless I stopped the caregiving. So I did that day. I cut him off entirely from my help, stopping any behaviors that only benefited him and not us. My decision was liberating.

That day, I realized another important lesson about healing. We are the only ones who suffer under the weight of expectation when another person's actions let us down. We suffer from disappointment, perhaps even anger. To alleviate our disappointment, we must adjust our expectations, aligning them to who the other person is, including their vulnerabilities and limitations—what they're reasonably capable of.

I also realized that my caregiving and excessive generosity, the second time, wasn't just financial. In both relationships, emotional support became one-way traffic that was insufficient to meet my needs. Though waning gradually toward the end of my marriage, this support was nonexistent. Emotional support from John also quickly became nonexistent. He either self-isolated as he consumed his alcohol or passed out drunk. He abandoned me almost entirely and almost every day.

His actions devastated me because it was his emotional support in the early part of our relationship—him meeting my needs—that had caused me to fall in love. But his support disappeared quickly as his own emotional needs and dysfunction took over and controlled him. As I told him repeatedly, "Love isn't enough."

When I look back on these two relationships and how I gave so much to individuals who were quite capable of taking care of themselves, I'm proud of my evolution and growth. I'm pleased that when I saw my behavior repeating, I learned the lesson and adjusted my behavior to suit my needs. The second time, with John, I could see myself giving so much to help despite often ignoring my own needs, and I could see that I wasn't getting what I needed in return. My vulnerability was crystal clear to me.

Although I'm aware of my extreme caregiver nature, I'm not entirely sure where it came from. This is an interesting nature versus nurture question.

When I was a child, my mother exhibited many of the same behaviors I did, so nurture may have played a role. I always felt like she was trying to compensate for something missing in certain people's lives—my dad's and my sister's, for example—through extensive caregiving. Perhaps she taught me caregiving to compensate for someone else's inability or shortcoming, to the detriment of self.

Alas, this trait is not all bad. Caregiving can be coupled with empathy and compassion, which, when used properly, are wonderful strengths. Empathy and compassion can dull the sharp, extreme edges when someone's vulnerabilities get the best of them. Most people need this empathy and compassion—along with help at times—to ease their suffering. However, this empathy mustn't spill over into losing oneself while assisting another.

Interestingly, I've never heard the word *caregiver* used to guide my spiritual work. Instead, I hear the words *healer* and *messenger*. Perhaps part of my life's work is to learn how to deliver my healing message without becoming so attached to others that I lose myself.

I Worked on Responding Rather than Reacting

Reacting, rather than responding, can be difficult and limiting for many survivors, including me. When we react, we engage with another person or situation angrily. I'll repeat another important lesson about healing: Anger sits inside of us and festers, even if only briefly. When we hold anger inside, it binds our hearts, preventing us from knowing love. Hate can do the same thing, perhaps more viscerally and for a more extended period. However, responding and engaging calmly and peacefully can prevent those negative feelings from ever settling into our being.

When I react, I create my own suffering. This activates my inner critic, wherein I pile trauma on myself. Reacting makes me mad at myself because I feel I should express myself more healthily. This anger at myself sits on top of my anger at the person or situation—all held within me. And I feel like shit. I disturb my peace, whereas my peace is something I'm desperately trying to keep as a mainstay of my life.

Learning to respond is hard as hell. Even with total presence and awareness of what is happening as a situation unfolds and contemplating how I want to respond, I can still react. Even when I know exactly why someone behaves the way they do, I can still be provoked into anger. In my defense, most behaviors that cause me to react today are extreme. The first time John called me a "f'ing c," I had an out-of-orbit, explosive reaction.

With focus, I'm getting better at responding as I continue to evolve and heal through self-discovery. Within a few months of practice, I responded to John by shrugging off his name-calling and walking away. Time will tell whether I can remain calm if I'm ever attacked verbally again in this same way.

I feel like I've been in the eye of a hurricane for some time now, allowing me to continue practicing and evolving. I'm calm in that eye but aware of the chaos churning and spinning around me. This is other people's chaos, however, intersecting with my life. Since the events happen to them directly and only indirectly or tangentially to me, I get opportunities to practice remaining calm and responding to their behavior. For example, if someone hurts my sister, I may want to react, but I know it's on her, not me, to react or respond. My opportunity is to help her choose how to respond.

I Met My Trauma-Response Types

Experts agree there are four trauma responses: fight, flight, freeze, and fawn. Before reading about trauma response, I had never heard of the *four* response types. Maybe you've heard of three—fight, flight, and freeze—but I had only heard of two: fight and flight. Neither resonated with me because they're not my predominant trauma response types, so I ignored that I might have a trauma response type at all.

I read about the "four Fs" in Pete Walker's book, and that's when I discovered I'm predominantly prone to a freeze/

fawn combination, with a little fight and occasional flight thrown in. My dissociative amnesia is clearly my freeze response, and I've already written about my extreme caregiving, embodying my fawn response. My occasional explosive anger when I react is me fighting when someone provokes me.

I've fled trauma twice in my lifetime. The first was moving to the US for college, and the second was moving to Hong Kong. The Hong Kong move best fits this description because it involved a conscious decision to leave my environment, whereas going to college was just part of growing up. But both presented opportunities to flee my difficult environments. When we moved so many times in my marriage, we fled our then-current environment, chasing that ever-elusive happiness.

I Discovered My Emotional Needs

Emotional needs are states or conditions that must be fulfilled to experience happiness and peace. We feel happy and content when our emotional needs are met and responded to appropriately. However, when they are not met, we can feel disconnected, unseen, and misunderstood.

During the early months of my trauma therapy work, Monica often asked about my emotional needs and whether I knew what they were. When she first asked me, I had no idea what she meant, and I'm sure I looked at her like she had two heads. Or maybe I was a deer in headlights. *Emotional needs? Huh?!*

One day, after several weeks of my quandary, she gave me a piece of paper listing what she said were "common" emotional needs.

"Here, see if this helps you. I don't normally do this, but I feel like you might need help since nothing seems to be coming to your mind," Monica said gently, in her empathetic way. "These are just ideas, terms people sometimes use to explain their emotional needs. Spend time with the words over the next week and see if anything resonates. No pressure and no biggie if they don't."

"Sure! You bet!" I joked, somewhat mocking myself.

I placed the paper on my night table, on top of the journal I wrote profusely in every day. Each morning and night, I stared forlornly at that piece of paper. Every time I looked at it, I willed just one word or phrase—*any* word or phrase—to jump off the page with jazz hands. A slight nod would have elated me immensely.

But nothing came. For several more weeks, not just the one week Monica suggested.

Then, one day, when Tristan and I were arguing, I was in my bedroom, near the night table, where that piece of paper had stared at me blankly for weeks. In the heat of the argument, as I glanced around the room and my eyes grazed the night table, four words *literally* jumped off the page. The letters were emblazoned as if in a witch's spell book, responding to an enchantment. Those words were *communication, acceptance,* and *unconditional love.*

Then it hit me: in the heat of our argument, we were not communicating. I already knew our emotional connection had waned some time ago—capped by spotty communication, which was mostly about the tactics of our lives together by then. Now we were fighting, brought on by my growth and healing and the release of my unhealthy emotions. But we still weren't communicating. I felt like he wasn't open to hearing me, which meant I could not communicate what was happening to me and to us.

Communication wasn't our only issue. That day, I finally understood why I had felt a void for so long in our relationship. I wasn't experiencing the acceptance and unconditional love I needed to be emotionally nurtured and whole. He rejected me that day and put his needs before mine, even though what I had asked for wasn't selfish, motivated by my ego, or unreasonable.

"Tristan, I'm trying to help us. I need you to have the same book learning about being a survivor that I've come to understand… why I act the way I act so that I can change and heal myself. I need you to do the same thing," I told him. "And I need you to get counseling through a trauma therapist so that you can process your own emotions and work on how that's impacted your life…how that's impacting us." I was pleading by this point.

"You know I've been working on my stuff in my own way," he replied. "Reading and counseling isn't going to do anything for me. That's your way, not my way, and not what I want to do." I think he may have been expressing his fear of going through the process I was in. Perhaps he knew how painful it would be for him.

At that moment, I realized that my feeling of rejection came from Tristan's inability to accept and love me unconditionally—to do what I needed him to do for us. He wasn't giving me what I needed.

Immediately upon knowing my emotional needs, I also knew he would most likely be unable to meet them in the future. That was the moment I knew our marriage wouldn't survive what I was going through. I knew his expectations and demands on me, and his placement of me somewhere between his second and fourth priority reflected his inability to meet my emotional needs.

As I began to scan our life and events, moving backward in our time together, I tried to but couldn't see many times when I felt my needs being met by him. I wasn't sure that these times existed. *Thirty years is a long time to be with someone, and maybe I felt something early on,* I told myself. Perhaps part of what drew me to him was our shared experiences as trauma survivors.

By the end of our relationship, communicating about the business of our life was limited to the *this, that, and the other* that must be done, mostly involving fulfilling some needs of our animals or property. We didn't talk about much else, at least not anything more than the superficial "fine" to the question, "How was your day?" We didn't talk about what we experienced nor how situations affected us. We rarely talked about our relationship or feelings. My emotions were put in my wall, mainly to keep the peace.

The physical distance between us over the years—as I traveled for my career and then we lived apart so much after I moved to Hong Kong—only exacerbated our emotional distance, even while sitting right next to each other. We were good about not going to our mobile phones to fill the void of conversation when in public, but we still often had long, sometimes awkward periods of silence between us.

Not only was daily communication increasingly limited, but the bigger problem came when I did express my feelings or views on something. I used to say we weren't in the same ballpark, but by the very end—when it came to splitting our assets and how much alimony I would pay—I felt like we weren't even on the same planet. He was somewhere on Mars with some of his ideas.

Our divergent realities became plainly clear in any discussion about why he had left me post-hypnotherapy. He would tell you he left Hong Kong to attend to his medical needs. To me, that was an awful enough reason for leaving me when he did, given his medical need was post-surgical physical therapy for a knee injury, which he was already getting in Hong Kong. In his mind, however, getting to his provider wasn't easy enough.

"Getting back and forth to PT is too hard. There's too much f'ing walking in Hong Kong, constantly going up and down f'ing hills or stairs. I need easier and faster access to PT without the hardship on my body," he explained, exerting his will. "You know the hospital in Thailand has both the hotel and a PT facility right there together."

"Alright, I understand that," I replied. "But the timing for me isn't great. There's a lot going on in my head."

"Yeah, but if I'm going to recover and get back to boarding by winter, I need to go now. Snow will start falling in Colorado in a couple of months."

It was July. And he wanted more convenient access to physical therapy to meet his need for snowboarding by November. He'd seen a glimpse of that convenience in the hospital in Thailand where he had surgery after his accident.

In my reality, he was running away from me. For all the five weeks post-hypnotherapy that we were physically together, I was an emotional wreck on a roller coaster of vacillating emotions as I processed my experience. Mostly during those weeks, I was inconsolably sad or very angry. I had a *really* hard time explaining what was happening to me. Whenever I tried to talk about it, his reaction was mostly about how it affected him. He would say, "You're scaring me," or "I don't know who you are," or "You're all over the place with your emotions." He never put his arms around me to console me or tell me I would be alright and that we would get through it—which is what I really wanted and needed. Instead, he sat across the table from me, his arms crossed, as he delivered his fears. Then he left me. I didn't see it then, but leaving me at such a vulnerable time after my life had shattered also displayed his lack of acceptance of, and unconditional love for, me.

Although I was in a quandary over his leaving me, and I wondered what was really going on, my caregiving nature meant that I didn't question him. In fact, I rationalized with him whether he would get better medical care in Colorado or Thailand, including considering the impact of the pandemic. I let him put himself before me. Emotionless again and allowing myself to be the last priority, I was in a familiar place.

Obviously, he had accepted me into his life, but there were so many things about me he didn't accept. I came to feel rejected, especially toward the end, but I realized I had bent from early in our relationship to get his acceptance. I had given up my independence and many things I needed to nurture my soul. I became almost subservient to his needs.

He rarely complimented me. I only felt beautiful on the rare occasion that he told me this, which came when I was at my thinnest and dressed up for some occasion. Sometimes, his actions or words made me feel like I needed to change, bending to his expectations. My weight was always under a microscope. My boobs were too small. I was getting wrinkles too quickly. And my "sex" bored him. On several occasions, his reactions to other women told me what he wanted—which physically was not me. And my inner critic used that subliminal messaging against me.

He also never complimented my intellect or success. Sometimes, I felt like he competed with me. And I only recall a couple of times when he expressed pride in my accomplishments. Well, sort of....

I had taken the exam to become a CPA several times, with each failure deflating me. I was immensely relieved the day that a big brown envelope came in the mail. It meant I had passed the exam and could go on to full certification. A regular, letter-sized envelope was never good news; I had received a few of those already. On this day, I fell to my knees. My pain of trying—which meant months of constant studying each time but failing—was finally over. Passing the exam was a big deal and a required access point to moving into the lucrative stages of my career.

"Good job. See, there are no quitters in this household," Tristan said simply.

I do believe Tristan loved me but in his own way. His love was more of a security detail—a "no one is ever going to hurt you" kind of love. He was a protector of my physical being, perhaps since I was his caregiver and provider, rather than a protector and nurturer of my heart. His inability to love me as I need to be loved, no matter who I was or what I was experiencing, became crystal clear in his response to me post-hypnotherapy.

We still communicate from time to time. Being amicable with each other is important to me as part of the neutral place we've established, wherein I neither love nor hate him. He's just a person who was once significant in my life. Sometimes, he asks for my advice, which I give by asking him questions to his questions, never telling him what to do. Never caregiving.

Recently, he asked me via text, "I'm weighing the pros and cons of selling the property in Conifer. Here are five things I'm considering. Is the Universe saying, 'Stay with your dreams, and I will help you,' or is it saying, 'You're chasing the wrong dream?' You know me better than anyone. Am I missing something?"

Everything on his list was a reason to sell, indicating he was chasing the wrong dream; this is a pattern that he'd long held true, in my opinion.

"What's saying 'stay with your dreams?'" I asked him.

"Not one thing you wrote says that to me."

"Thanks, that really impacted me. You are right, not one thing," he replied.

To this day, despite still having a relationship, we haven't discussed what happened in my hypnotherapy session. Nor have we discussed what I've learned about my past traumas, nor what I've learned about who I am and my life purpose. Most likely, we never will talk about any of this.

When John came into my life, almost one year to the day post-hypnotherapy, I felt acceptance and unconditional love almost immediately. Because I was learning so quickly—already healing, rapidly evolving, and seeing the effect of my healing—I was like a geyser gushing out so much of my story. He was a great listener. Much of what I shared was difficult to hear and painted a very different picture of me than the one he had in his mind, but he still accepted everything I told him. He accepted *me*. I never felt like damaged goods with him.

Despite the short duration of our relationship, I was given a taste of what communication, acceptance, and unconditional love feel like, and I learned that's what I need from an intimate partner. Having my emotional needs met is crucial to being a whole person and thriving in life. After knowing what it's like not to have my needs met, I will never be in a relationship like that again.

The day I discovered my emotional needs was one of the most defining days of my healing journey so far. Not only was it the day I understood what Monica had talked about for so many weeks, but it was also when I understood how deprived I had been for so long. I had sadness at my deprivation but also joy in the self-discovery. I had joy because, for the first time, I understood what I needed emotionally by seeing clearly what wasn't working for me. It was a moment of recognizing the opposites—the void I was used to feeling as opposed to knowing something much more sustaining.

Oddly enough, despite my frustration with myself as my self-discovery evolved, I didn't have negative feelings toward myself. I accepted enough truth about my past to give myself a lot of grace. I understood I couldn't identify my emotional needs because they had rarely been met, even in my most significant relationships.

I looked back over my life to see whether I had ever experienced what I needed. College is where I remember feeling accepted. I joined Chi Omega Women's Fraternity and Greek life during my first week of college. Despite proclaiming to be "from Indonesia," and almost everyone recognizing the English-looking girl wasn't fully American, no one cared about my name, my family, or where I came from. They accepted me for me, with all my quirks.

My fraternity sisters still love me unconditionally. As I have publicly told my story, these women have been some of my strongest supporters.

I also know I was accepted and loved unconditionally by my Aunt Cheeto, mostly because of the person she was. But I do wonder whether it also had something to do with our shared experience, although I'm not sure she knew about it. Whether or not she knew doesn't matter. What matters is she made me feel accepted and loved because I was "my Bethie, Cheeto's baby girl."

I see acceptance and unconditional love today as I continue engaging in relationships with my parents, Natalie, and her kids. The cool thing is my family also sees my ability to accept them and love them unconditionally. I now regularly hear comments like "I've never experienced unconditional love like I do with you" from some family members. This strongly confirms my ability to give and receive love. This is the Universe touching me again and telling me I'm *exactly* where I'm meant to be today.

I Accepted My Strengths and Gifts

When I began trauma therapy post-hypnotherapy, for the most part, I couldn't tell you what my strengths and gifts were, mostly because of my imposter syndrome and the loud, obnoxious voice of my inner critic. For those of us plagued with this reality, discovering our strengths and gifts can be very beneficial to shushing that voice in our head. Admitting our strengths and gifts, saying the words aloud or in writing, is even more powerful because it plays up our self-worth and helps us see the incredible human beings we are. So, I will acknowledge some of my strengths and pump myself up!

I am strong, resilient, and courageous, all strengths forged by who I am and my life experiences. I see my own strength as I've persevered through my darkest and most difficult times. There were many months when it took every ounce of my strength to get out of bed and face whatever the day held for me. Healing, as I've done, isn't for the faint of heart.

I've heard repeatedly as I've told my story that I am resilient and have courage. Personal storytelling is one of my gifts, and almost everyone gives me positive reinforcement about my courage and what I'm doing to help others heal by sharing my story publicly. These welcome messages push back against my inner critic, especially because I hear them from outside. I believe them.

I've already written about being a natural problem-solver, best exemplified when I took charge of my own healing process after crashing into my wall. Finally, I used my gift to help myself. Since problem-solving came naturally to me, I never saw this as a strength until I began my self-discovery work. Maybe I ignored that part, focusing instead on my problem-solving when it came to helping others and almost never myself.

As I mentioned, I knew I was a natural problem-solver through my professional work to solve a company's problem, including through leading teams in this process. Sometimes, a project lasted for years and included multiple work streams and teams worldwide in different disciplines. Our course of action planned at the beginning of an investigation was never the same path we took to get to the end because we had to adjust as facts were uncovered. For years, one of my primary roles was to help my teams redirect our work to overcome these problems.

More recently, as I've come to understand myself as a teacher and healing mentor, I see the other help I've provided to my colleagues—mentoring and counseling them through their own personal struggles. I've offered them alternative strategies and processes to consider, often personal and involving that ever-elusive work-life balance. I've helped them with decisions about self-advocacy, focusing on family first, who to talk to for help with managing their commitments and responsibilities, how to message their needs to coaches and leaders, when to take a leave of absence, and so on....

I'm also highly adaptable and mostly unresistant to change. This strength and gift served me well in surviving, but it also still profoundly serves me as I'm going through my biggest transformation, moving from my first to my second mountain. Over the past four years during this move, my life has been embedded with many significant life changes. I know changes like this can challenge most people, and I feel fortunate that I've been able to navigate them seamlessly and without hesitation.

Once I began to look at my life events, it was no surprise to me to discover how adaptable and unresistant I had become to change. Change is the only constant in this world, as the saying goes, and those shifts began for me at an early age, growing up in an expatriate family. I lived in six different cities before I turned eighteen.

My gift of adaptability showed up again during those years of chaos as an adult. Tristan and I had homes and/or lived in ten different cities during our thirty years together. Each of these came with new challenges and circumstances to adapt to.

One of my most significant adaptations to change was when I became the sole financial provider in my marriage, a pressure that made me feel trapped, like a hamster spinning on a wheel. My feelings hit an all-time high in a dramatic way when I entered 2021, paying the housing costs in five locations in this world. This included the outrageous cost for our three properties in the US, two with mortgages, my rent in Hong Kong, and Tristan's residence in the W Hotel in Thailand.

Eight months after my hypnotherapy, Tristan and I made the decision to part ways. Our divorce was final less than one year later. The enormity of the financial burden had crushed me. It took eighteen months to resolve, but I was free of most of that burden by the end of 2022.

Concurrent with receiving our final divorce decree, I left Hong Kong and moved back to Texas, almost on a spur-of-the-moment decision. I moved to a part of the world I thought I would never live in again, uprooting myself from friends in Hong Kong who had become part of my support team. Working in a different city also meant I essentially changed jobs, though I remained with the same company.

Once in Texas, I reclaimed many of my relationships with family and friends. I experienced found-and-lost love again with who I thought was my life partner. Now, I'm moving on to do my work as a teacher and healing mentor. This career change will impact how I provide a roof over my head as I become self-employed.

Fierce independence is another strength that has served me well throughout my life, but I must not misuse it against myself. There's not much I cannot do for myself, including tending to my emotions. But for a long time, my strength of independence contributed to living quite comfortably behind my wall. For me, independence also meant great comfort in my solitude. As I buried myself deeper and deeper behind my wall, I found peace there. Yes, I was alone and lonely, but often at peace. Because I avoided conflict and drama, I found comfort in this peace, enabling me to remain right where I was.

However, independence and finding peace in solitude didn't mean I wouldn't need help. I've now evolved enough to know when I need to ask for help, and I know where to get it. I don't need the "damsel in distress" or the "I'll kill anyone who hurts you" kind of help some people have tried to give me. Nor the self-motivated "guidance" others have offered me. Rather, now I have a support team who nurtures me when I ask.

While I don't "do life" alone anymore, I do use my independence to ensure I'm never dependent on anyone for anything. The freedom to do what I want when I want, to make decisions entirely based on my needs, and to be unapologetically me is liberating! I can care for myself, but I'm so much better when I do this by seeking help and guidance from others when I need it. And while I can choose to take care of only myself, I relish my freedom now to choose when and how I help others.

Being open-minded is the strength that enables me to try every healing tool that comes my way. Regarding people, I'm accepting of everyone without judgment. This most certainly comes from my multicultural life experiences.

My open-mindedness affects how I evaluate my relationships with people who have hurt me, as I decide what to do with them. I'll talk more about this later, but for now, I'll just say the power of being open-minded comes from the idea that *people who hurt us are a lot like us.*

Being open-minded is also a useful gift as I work with others to help them heal because I have no preconceived ideas about who someone is, why they are who they are, why they behave as they do, or how they will heal—or whether they will heal, for that matter. We each walk our own path, and I accept wherever anyone else's path goes.

I Found My Life's Purpose

Purpose is a concept I've wrestled with for many years, going back to well before my hypnotherapy. I recall thinking about this a lot through the years, but I am shocked at how long

I have struggled with this. As I researched for this book, I found something I must have written back in the Spring of 2014—a document called "Disrupted Life"—which reflects my thoughts back then about searching for my purpose. Finding my purpose was a "current disruption," I wrote. I went on to describe what I now see as the beginnings of my self-evolution in this area:

> *I think this topic resonated with me so much because of the current disruption in my life—my quest to find my true purpose in life. I find myself sitting back and watching various events coming together now, which seem to be paving the path forward. Not sure where it will end up, but perhaps for the first time in my life…I find the loud but persistent beating of the drum pointing me in a new direction.*
>
> *For several years, I have wondered, sometimes with some level of despair, what my life's purpose is. I can't be on this Earth simply to go to work every day and earn a paycheck, wander toward retirement, and die. This seems so unfulfilling to me and perhaps misses the mark on what I am meant to do. These thoughts have come from my understanding that in each lifetime, we are meant to learn something that we failed to learn in a previous lifetime, all to the end of moving the soul toward finding our higher spiritual selves. If that's the case, then what am I meant to learn or do in this lifetime?*

I had a revelation earlier this year that at least part of this life's purpose is to support another human being—Tristan—on his journey to find his true purpose in this lifetime. He has tremendous spiritual capability but seems to have a hard time harnessing the power of his capability because of so many constant disruptions that he also experiences and is forever trying to deal with and understand. We've been together for more than half of our lives, so many of the disruptions we have shared together; others we have experienced separately, but the commonality of our separate experiences is striking (though we are very different people).

This revelation was the starting point of my current more significant disruption—a building drumroll to what I think (hope) will be a thunderous conclusion.... Realizing that supporting him on his journey is one of my life's purposes and...I'm okay with that. But there must be something more for ME.

Of course, I had no idea back then what lay ahead of me, but I knew there must be more to life than earning a paycheck and supporting someone else through their life. I could see then that I was meant for more, but my focus was on Tristan because he was all I could see then. Looking back now and reading what I wrote, I think I was trying to get okay with my reality, but clearly, I was really searching for *ME*. I left for Hong Kong in 2016, around eighteen months after I wrote that passage.

When my spiritual journey led me to astrology that same year, that, too, was about trying to understand my life's purpose. I asked myself, *Who am I? What is my purpose?* And only found unsatisfying answers. To each answer, I would then question, *Really, Universe, is that it?*

In the intervening years—wherein I moved toward my moment of spontaneous combustion—my focus on me and my purpose became more intense. The drumming intensified, beating faster and faster and louder and louder. My attempt to accept what I thought was my purpose eventually led me to complete dissatisfaction, and the nearer I drew to the dividing line of my life, the more I became exasperated.

My exasperation peaked just before my hypnotherapy. I was being crushed under the weight of a massive boulder I was carrying up a mountain, but I didn't know why. My understanding of so many things about myself took a radical turn that day in hypnotherapy.

But I didn't immediately understand. In the early weeks after hypnotherapy, as I looked back at how purpose had played out in my life, all I could see was Tristan. I would forlornly ask myself the dreaded question I had no answer to: *Is that all I'm meant to do in this life?* Now, I know my vulnerability as an extreme caregiver was getting in the way, too, of seeing beyond him.

In a wonderful example of my pathway unfolding before me, my self-discovery about my life's purpose—being a teacher and healing mentor—began by telling people I would "find my voice." After coming through a painful time as I progressed with trauma therapy, I began to have the pulling urge to speak up about how liberating healing had been for me. I wanted to shout at the top of my voice the good news that *survivors can heal and find freedom from unhealthy survivorship*. But I had trouble finding the right words. So, I would simply tell people I would "find my voice."

The words that did come out were often jubilant because of my many touches of the Universe by then. My words were rejected, however, on more than one occasion by members of TALK at group meetings. So, too, were my words rejected by Tristan.

At first, I was shocked by their rejection, but I quickly realized two things. First, all those people weren't ready to—or couldn't—see themselves finding the joy I felt. They weren't ready to heal like I was. It wasn't their time.

Second, I realized my words weren't on point to help those people. My words were an expression of how I felt at the time, but they didn't embody what I had been through to get to where I was. Nor did my words show empathy for the pain and suffering that other survivors around me were still living with. My words needed refinement to crystallize my message to my community.

One day, I reconnected with a friend who I hadn't talked to in around five years. I told him what I knew about my abuse and how I was surviving.

"You know, I need to introduce you to my fourth-grade girlfriend who I just reconnected with because I think you have a lot in common," he replied.

Boy, do we ever! She has been through similar abuse to mine; she is also a survivor; she is a Texas girl who lived in Singapore for a while, and...she wrote her story in a book titled *Finding Your Voice: A Path to Recovery for Survivors of Abuse* by Mannette Morgan. Do you think I've read it?! Indeed, I have! I couldn't get my hands on it fast enough after he told me about her!

Since then, finding my voice has been about developing my message to teach and mentor others based on my experiences. That all began with a wonderful organization called Lightbeamers, which I found through social media while looking for direction. The founder of Lightbeamers is a master storyteller, encouraging people to use the power of their personal stories to amplify their brands, grow their businesses, and shine their lights to bring good to the world. For this last reason (I discovered that, astrologically, I was born to bring light to dark), I was drawn to see whether she could help me harness the power of my story.

I spent a day with this woman, pouring out the details of my life as I understood it then. Almost instantly, she urged, "You have an incredible story that belongs in this book I'm going to publish next year, full of inspirational stories just like yours. You've been so brave, and the world needs to hear this. We're beginning work early next year, so your timing is impeccable!"

And so, I did. I stepped into my brave and wrote the *CliffsNotes* version of my story.

Step Into Your Brave: Uplifting Stories to Inspire Courage, Strength, and Growth, by April Adams Pertuis (I refer to this book herein as "SIYB"), was published in October 2022. April is the founder of Lightbeamers. April is also my fraternity sister, whom I have known for thirty-five years. Before that day we spent together post-hypnotherapy, we had only superficial contact with one another through social media. When we first met all those years ago, we were just two silly college girls doing what college girls do. Neither of us dreamed back then that all these years later, our paths would cross again in such a profound way.

Finding Lightbeamers and publishing in SIYB helped me harness the power of my story and dip my toe into sharing my experiences—some of which are difficult to speak and hear about—in a public forum. I intended to engage with people who needed to know my story, but at the time, writing one chapter in SIYB was enough for me. One. And. *Done!*

Since then, I've told my story verbally to many family members, friends, and colleagues who have read SIYB. I shared my story in fireside chats throughout the organization I worked for, and I've met and connected with people from all over the world who I may or may not have known previously. They all want to talk after they hear me share. SIYB is an Amazon international best-seller, which has expanded my audience to people I don't know. Some of them I've now met because they, too, are talking.

And remember why TALK exists? When I spoke publicly on that radio program with Taura, that's when I began to find my voice.

Discovering Lightbeamers and contributing to SIYB has helped me manifest what I know as my purpose. Talking with Monica about my views on forgiveness moved me forward on my path to writing this book, which I know is meant to help me connect my healing message with that larger community I need to reach. I also met my writing and publishing coach while working on the SIYB project. She was part of the powerhouse duo of women, along with my friend, who brought that book to life.

I now see the unfolding of a beautiful, divinely led path I'm on. I've experienced all my life events for reasons that I now know have been feeding my purpose since the day I was born.

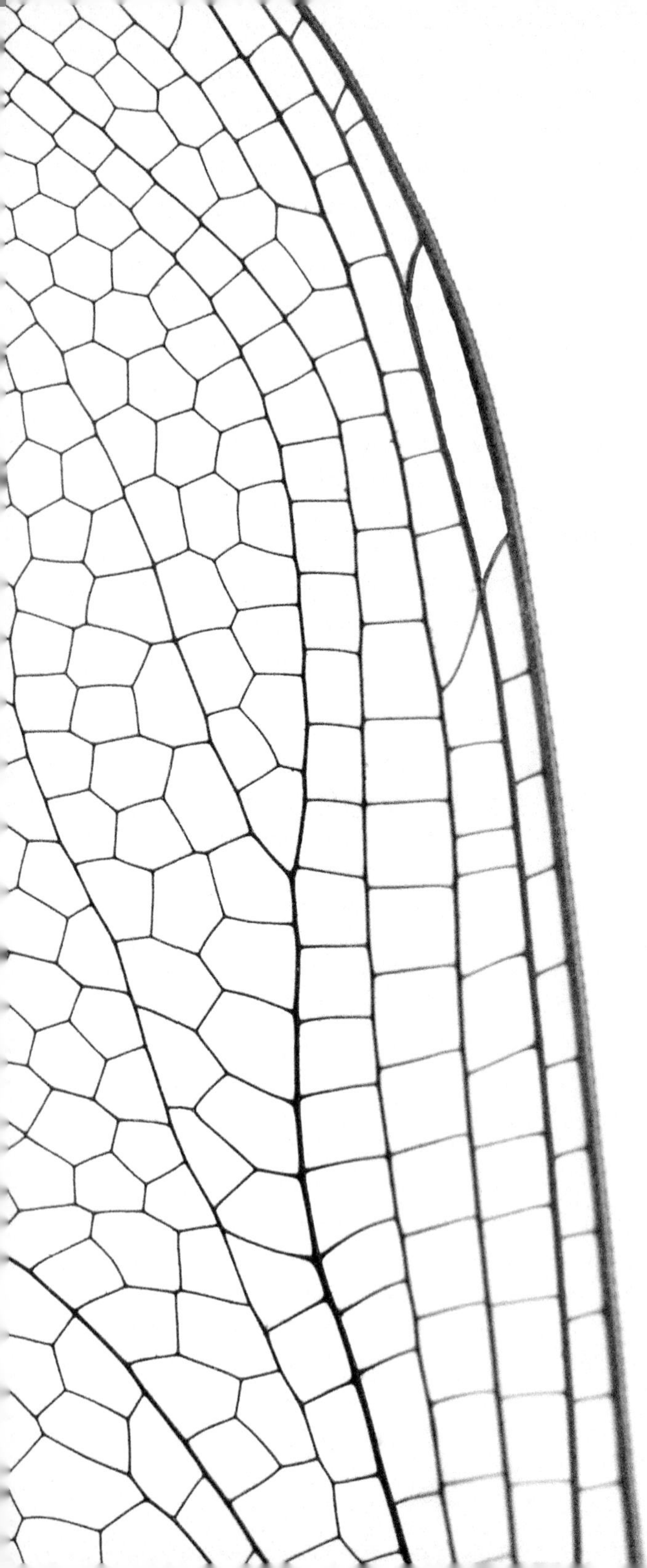

CHAPTER 8

LEARNING TO MIRROR

THIS CHAPTER IS short because the concept I'll discuss is simple. If you can grasp the concept, mirroring may help you resolve some of your most hurtful relationships.

I found grace for and acceptance of myself as a survivor by learning why and how I had lived behind my wall. Discovering there are four trauma response types—including the two most relevant to me—was paramount to understanding myself and the *how* and the *why* of my wall. Knowing their existence as common response types and the behaviors associated with each was liberating for me. This awareness marked another moment when the Universe touched me.

But I benefited most from this process when I learned to see myself reflected in those who had hurt me, viewing both of us as survivors.

Today, I have few remaining judgments about myself. I understand that all of my life's experiences have shaped me. Explanations exist for the choices I made and the way I behaved as I survived. If this is true for me, then it's also true for every other survivor living with unhealthy survivorship.

As I process the trauma and my hurt associated with people close to me, this same grace for and acceptance of them emerges from me. While I may never know *why* they behave as they do, I do understand the source driving the part of them that hurt me is most likely trauma and the manifestation of their experiences. They are likely just trying to survive the effect of their own unprocessed trauma and suffering. Seeing them as I see myself is what I refer to as "mirroring."

Mirroring helps us reframe our understanding of others. By understanding more about *self* and how we interact in our significant relationships, we can mirror our understanding toward the other person. When our interactions are challenging or difficult, mirroring helps answer the question, "Why did you hurt me?"

Someone else's unhealthy survivorship intersecting with ours in an unhealthy way is no different from our own unhealthy survivorship intersecting with others—prompting actions and reactions. If we can perform a *parentectomy,* thereby causing our parents pain in our absence, or if we cuss at someone in anger, causing them to feel as if they don't matter, then someone else's survivorship can also come back on us in an unhealthy way. In the same way we react to what happened to us, they, too, might be reacting to what happened to them.

Owning my own behavior and understanding its cause brings my interactions full circle. When bad behavior is directed at me, I can tell myself, *That behavior is yours, not mine.* I can see it for what it is and where it may emanate from, but I don't take it on as my own. I simply give it back to them. "Yours, not mine," are words I have spoken.

Mirroring and finding grace for and acceptance of someone who hurt me, without judgment, and being open-minded to them as a human being is how I let go of any negative emotions in my heart, whether anger or hatred. Those negative emotions no longer serve me, and if I held them, they would only constrain me and hold me back from what I'm seeking, which, as you know by now, is *love*.

Letting go of my emotions doesn't mean I'm accepting their behavior. If what I'm experiencing in my interactions with the other person isn't working for me, I get to choose what to do with the relationship and how to continue engaging with that person—or not—based on what's best for me. When I make these decisions, I'm driven by self-love first. And I know the importance of healing in the relationship before deciding whether and how I will continue to engage.

Today, I make these decisions from that healed place and for the right reasons, but this hasn't always been the case for me. I'm much healthier today, which is the difference. I've done the work to heal much of the hurt in some of my most serious and important relationships, including with myself. I've even healed the pain of my relationships with my grandfather, Tristan, and John.

What I call mirroring might be what some people call forgiveness, or at least a part of the process of forgiving. Early in this book, I wrote that I would have dismissed anyone who told me I must forgive to heal before I began this part of my healing journey. I still might dismiss this today. But by healing myself and mirroring my healing onto others, I've been able to simply let go. And I've never needed to utter the words "I forgive you" to do so.

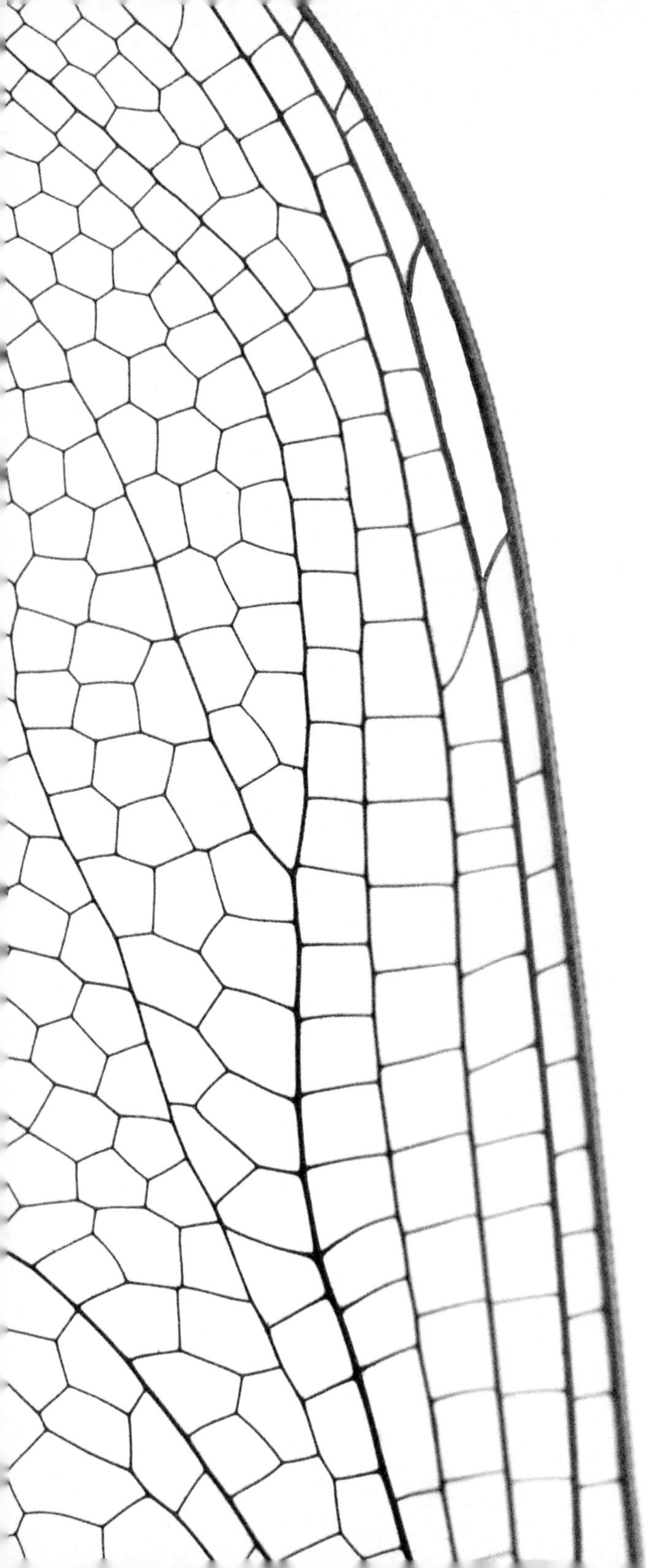

CHAPTER 9

REFRAMING THE HARDEST PARTS

MANY OF MY most serious and important relationships have taken me on a journey of trauma and unhealthy survivorship. Yet, through my healing, I've evolved in how I see these people. I now recognize that the survivor in me is also in them. I can best demonstrate this transformation by describing my healing process in relation to my grandfather, my first abuser.

Being a Jones meant I was born to a family with elders who commanded *respect*. Respect was a birthright, an obligation, not something earned. And this expectation remained no matter what the elder did.

For example, I grew up automatically saying "yes sir" and "no ma'am" without hesitation. Those words were expected. Otherwise, I would suffer the consequences of a stern reprimand.

"Does it break your jaw to say 'no sir'?" This was uttered more than a few times in my life. None of my elders considered why I might withhold respect in a situation.

Receiving respect was a particularly acute desire for my dad; he expected it to be displayed toward my mom and him. But my grandparents expected it even more so. Showing respect thus became a conditioned response, even when I didn't feel like it.

I was never a rude, bratty kid; that wasn't me. Rather, I felt like my respect was misplaced—unearned and undeserved. As the saying goes, "You don't throw stones from inside glass houses." Or said my way, "You don't respect me, so why should I respect you?" Although I didn't know it, that mantra must have lived inside of me even in childhood.

Displaying *love and affection* for family members was also expected. Sometimes, I gave hugs and kisses because I was expected to. This was more difficult for me than displaying respect for two reasons.

First, I grew up living halfway around the world from my extended family, including my grandparents, and only saw them for a few weeks each year, usually in the summertime. We had snail mail and sometimes telephone calls, but my interaction with them was limited. We never had time to develop our relationship until after I graduated from high school and moved back to the United States. They were almost strangers to me when I moved back to Texas to go to college.

The other reason I found it more difficult to display affection than respect is because respect can be shown mostly through words, with no physical contact. Displaying love, or at least affection, requires physical contact. That always felt uncomfortable for me with my grandfather. For years, I thought it was because he was such a large, towering man, gruff in his ways, and he scared me. Now, of course, I know my fear came from being abused by him. I feigned love and affection for my grandparents, often uncomfortably giving in to the pressure of their expectations.

When I returned to Texas for college, I moved back by myself. I had extended family nearby—in fact, that's one of the reasons why I ended up at this school—but my parents and sister remained in Indonesia. I had almost no experience being an American, let alone developing from a teenager into an adult in American ways, so I needed help. Although my Aunt Cheeto tried to teach me in the summers when I visited her, I hadn't yet learned basic living tasks for an emerging adult, like cooking or not overdrawing my bank account.

Before college, I had never had a bank account or any restrictions on spending. My parents believed, quite accurately, that I might need a little guardianship when I moved back.

A few funny stories happened during my first few months in Texas during my freshman year of college, illustrating why I needed help. One of my mom's favorite stories on this topic is about me continually overdrawing my bank account.

"Why do you keep doing that?" my mom asked over the telephone.

"Well, I still have checks," I told her. So I thought I could just keep writing them. Ha!

Another time, a check bounced on my account because I let one of my fraternity sisters sign it. This might have been okay had she forged my name, but she signed hers instead. The bank rejected the check. Luckily for me, this small bank in East Texas was also where my grandparents did business and were well-known, and the bank's president was my dad's childhood friend. My parents, grandparents, and the bank's president had many discussions about my behavior. Rather than the normal bank penalties one might expect, the bank and my family treated the situation as a learning experience for me. Truth be told, the bank would have been completely reasonable had they closed my account.

I also literally couldn't boil water. One night, I put water on the stove for macaroni and cheese, but then I left the kitchen for a telephone call with a friend. When I went back downstairs after the call ended, there was no water in the pot, and the pan had begun to glow red with heat. That might have been the phone call where my dad went into orbit when he got the telephone bill. I had no appreciation for the cost of long-distance calls to other countries back then. The glowing red of the pot gives some indication of the length and cost of that call.

Do you see? My parents were right; I needed some guidance!

My grandparents served as my guardians—not legally, but that was their role when my parents weren't in the United States. When I left campus, I spent my weekends and holidays with my grandparents. They took care of me, ensuring I had what I needed—feeding me, helping me with my laundry, and allowing me to sleep when needed.

During this time, I discovered, or perhaps re-discovered, my grandfather's predatory eyes, which scared the hell out of me. Sometimes, when our eyes locked, the eyes staring back at me showed me that I was the prey—like the classic wolf in the wild staring down a rabbit on a *National Geographic* wildlife show. The hair on my body stood on end when I saw those eyes.

I forgot about his predatory eyes for many, many years, perhaps because they died with him in 1994. By then, I was in my mid-twenties, a couple of years into my marriage and career. But all the unprocessed trauma associated with him—and his eyes—remained inside of me. The way I coped contributed to my wall.

I didn't think about him after he died until I recalled being abused by him when my Aunt Cheeto told her truth some ten years later. Ironically, I had no idea he was still stalking me, like prey, in my subconscious mind through my nightmare.

Then, in the early stages of my trauma therapy, post-hypnotherapy, the memory of his eyes entered my conscious mind with a vengeance, bringing back my fear. My fear of him, along with my other emotions stemming from his abuse, was one of the first traumas I worked on processing with Monica. Those eyes, which I realized were seared into my memory but pushed to the dark recesses of my mind, had to go.

After intense EMDR therapy work with Monica and facing those eyes head-on, my mind finally released its fear. The image in my mind changed to something much less scary. Now, when I think about him, I see the toy googly eyes that sometimes appear on stuffed animals. In my mind, they're spinning around, all crazy-like, which amuses me. His eyes no longer have power over me.

During the time I worked to heal from my fear of my grandfather, I was reading Pete Walker's book *Complex PTSD: Surviving to Thriving*. I made note of certain behaviors I saw in myself, but I also noted other significant people with whom I've struggled in relationships. My notes in the margins on these pages are profuse. *Me. Me. Me. There is my mom! That might be my dad! Oh, look, there is Tristan!*

My grandfather is there too. I began to align his behavior with what I already knew to be a line of generational, familial abuse on that side of my family. I considered that my grandfather abused others, including me, because he was abused or traumatized in some way himself. I wasn't giving him an excuse or forgiving him for what he did to me. Rather, I began to see him as a wounded human being, suffering under the weight of his own life experiences, just like I was. Yes, he was the starting point for my abuse and trauma, but having processed many of my negative emotions associated with him by then, I was beginning to mirror for the first time. I was beginning to find grace for and acceptance of him so that I could let him go.

My therapeutic work to process the trauma my grandfather inflicted on me took some time. Dealing with his eyes was the culmination of much work. But I did it despite my pain and fear. I healed my emotions and my negative "I" statements associated with him.

As I mentioned, he died in 1994, long before I began my focused and intentional healing work. Had he been alive while I was going through this part of my healing journey, I honestly cannot say what I would have done with the relationship. Continuing as it was became impossible, given my release of his power over me. Whether I would have exiled him or continued our relationship with new boundaries, I cannot say.

In the next section of this book, I will talk about my relationship with my parents and how that evolved over time, which is a beautiful story. Punch line: they are out of exile now, and we are in a healthier relationship, with my boundaries intact. So, who knows? Perhaps I would have come to a beautiful, healed place with my grandfather too.

The story involving my parents is beautiful partly because they have done their own work to allow us to heal and move past barriers that we all needed to overcome. I don't know whether my grandfather could have done similar work, which would have required him to own his behavior. I think that would have been quite difficult when his behavior harmed another being. As ugly and destructive as his behavior has been in multiple generations of my family, owning it may have been impossible for him.

My relationship was with a man who had died and couldn't participate in my healing work. Still, that, to me, was a crucial and important lesson from my healing process. Knowing I can heal relationships with people who have hurt me without their participation is powerful. He could never apologize to me with words or through actions because he's gone. I don't need his apology anyway. I've been able to evolve my thinking about him, allowing me to let go of his actions' effect on me. He has little hold on me today. I'm not sure the hurt ever goes completely away, but I healed the relationship sufficiently so that it stopped constraining me from knowing love.

Everything to this point—evolving my thinking about my grandfather—was enough to heal. But this is where things got *really* weird, as my thinking continued to evolve—and still does. Recently, I read a book about forgiveness called *Radical Forgiveness: A Revolutionary Five-Stage Process to Heal Relationships, Let Go of Anger and Blame, and Find Peace in Any Situation* by Colin Tipping. This title piqued my interest while researching books on forgiveness. I will explain in my own words why the book has "radical" in its title, using what happened to me as I continued to evolve my thinking about my grandfather.

I'm a longtime believer, as Tipping seems to be, in the idea that our souls travel through many lifetimes. In each lifetime, we're learning what we must and living our life's purpose, moving towards ultimate enlightenment, perhaps heaven, at the end of our final physical life. Some souls are part of our *soul pack*, and we travel with them throughout our lifetimes, each playing different roles as we travel. People we encounter each lifetime are at various places in their soul's journey toward enlightenment. Some are more evolved and enlightened than others.

We have a purpose in each of our lives, regardless of whether we ever know it. Although it took me over fifty years to figure out mine, I know this is because I needed to experience certain events to help others heal. I had to suffer, live with my unhealthy survivorship, walk my healing journey, and experience hope, evolution, and love. Suffering because of my grandfather was a part of fulfilling my life's purpose.

Now for the weird part. If I believe my soul is on a journey, which I do, then Tipping asks me to accept something very, very radical. He asks me to believe my soul knew its purpose in this lifetime and *willingly* came into this life. Ergo, my soul chose for me to be abused and chose my grandfather as my first abuser. When my soul incarnated into my current physical form, we made a soul pact that he would be the one. Hold on…it gets weirder. Since this is what my soul *chose*, there's nothing to forgive. Now *that* is a wicked-radical belief. Radical forgiveness, indeed!

Wtf?! My mind scrambled the first, second, and third time I read what Tipping asked me to consider. But I knew I was drawn to read this book because it was another step on my pathway to healing and helping others. If I could accept this about my grandfather, I could be completely free of him.

I'm not suggesting you or anyone else must get to this place to heal a harmful relationship. Rather, I tell you this story to illustrate how far I've come in healing this most difficult relationship and in the evolution of my thinking. Also, I'm trying to find the good in my relationship with someone who hurt me so deeply and profoundly. And I'm seeking genuine gratitude for the relationship and what it taught me.

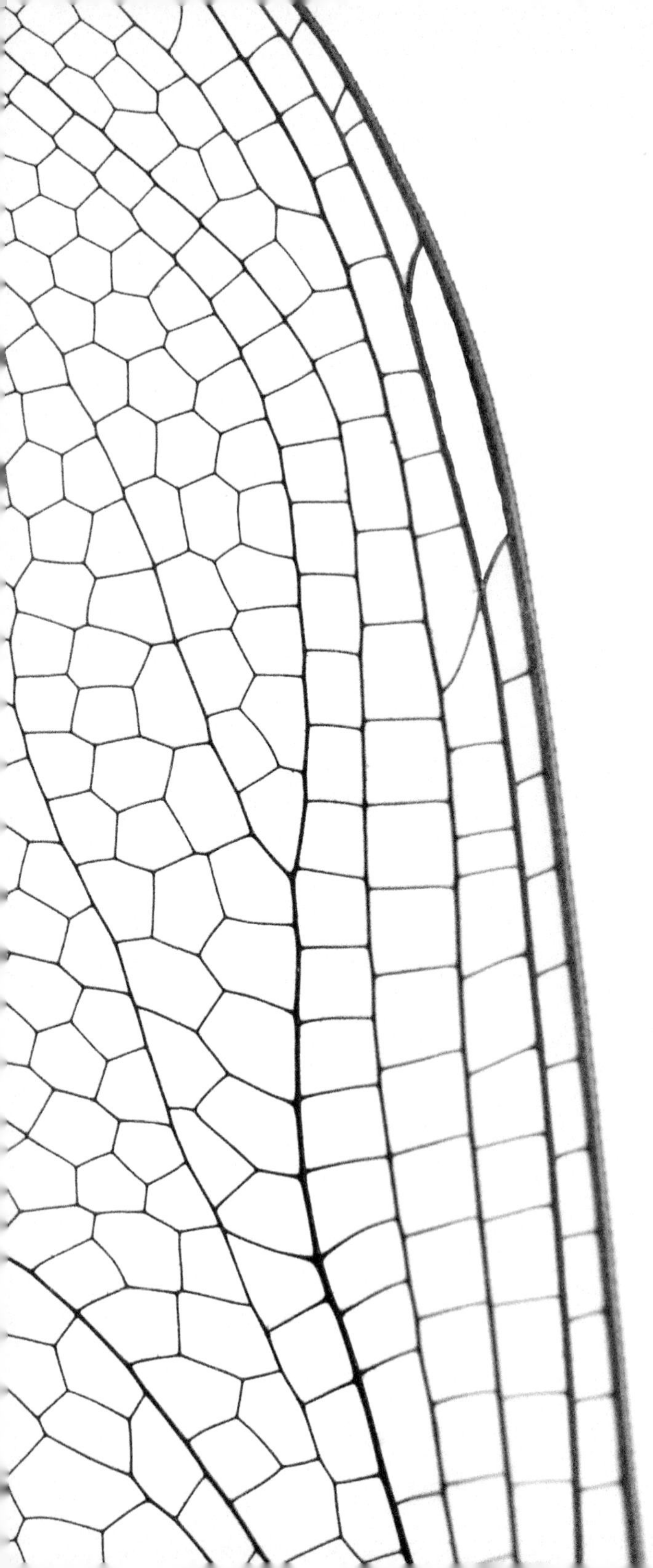

PART IV
—
LOVE

Love is my "L" in HEAL because love is our greatest gift to ourselves in the healing process. We must heal to get love right. When we heal, love ignites our soul, bringing joy and meaning to our existence.

LOVE SEEMS TO be as misunderstood as forgiveness. Many of us don't know what love is, where it comes from, or how we sustain it. Our life experiences shape what we know about love, and because of mine, I was confused. If you think about it, really think about it, you may be perplexed, too.

My confusion began when I was five years old because I was abused by someone who I thought loved me. Mirroring helped me realize perhaps he had never experienced real love. He certainly didn't know how to give and receive love healthily to me.

I grew up in a household where the expression of love was perplexing. I know my parents loved each other, but I rarely, if ever, saw their love demonstrated. Mostly, I remember they fought. My dad's unhealthy behavior was often the cause, and my mom was sad. For years as an adult, I couldn't understand why they were still together. But today, they've been married for more than fifty-five years. Spending time with them now, I no longer think it's the force of habit that keeps them together. Rather, I know there is love.

My dad's journey as a cycle breaker meant there was little physical touch between me and him. Our minimal physical interactions almost felt robotic and obligatory for a parent/child, not emotionally nurturing. I hugged my dad as part of a daily routine, like at bedtime, but I don't recall spending much time with him beyond that—like talking and getting fatherly advice, for example.

The expression of love I remember most while growing up was through giving material possessions. This was the "love language" permeating our immediate family. There wasn't anything material I wanted growing up that my parents didn't give me. Yet I still wasn't getting my emotional needs met or being loved as I now know I needed.

My experiences with love through friendship also took a series of blows. In high school, my close circle of friends was limited, and some of them abandoned me in the crowd that bullied me after I was date-raped. Eventually, the boys quit trying to date me because they knew that any relationship would only last for a short period of time. Then, add in my home environment, where we rarely talked about anything remotely related to sex. Altogether, my traumatic and almost nonexistent experience with teenage dating prevented me from learning what healthy love from a partner might look like.

Then, I experienced my marriage, which I've already described. Over time, that essential part of love—having my emotional needs met—eroded to a point where my feelings about Tristan were unrecoverable. When he left for Thailand and chose himself entirely over me, I felt completely rejected.

When it came time for me to heal, you can see why I was confused about love.

Today, I know that having one's emotional needs met comes from many relationships, in part or whole. But for much of my life, I looked for love in all the wrong places, even though I turned to the *right* people by most norms: friends, family, and spouse. The problem, once again, is that these people were all shaped by their own experiences, many of them as survivors, which made them incapable of loving me as I needed.

This is one of our truths as survivors. Quite often, it's the most significant relationships in our lives that hurt us deeply. Once we've evolved in our own healing and understanding of who we are, we become much more equipped to intentionally interact in healthy ways. But this is difficult while living with unhealthy survivorship.

Ultimately, in our healing process, we must decide how we're going to engage with these relationships:

- We may stay in the relationship as it is.
- We may exit the relationship.
- Or we may modify the relationship with boundaries better suited to our needs.

I will explore each of these options through my experience with certain significant relationships in my life. What is common for me in each experience is that love, led by self-love and my desire for closeness with people who meet my emotional needs, has driven each decision.

My Quest for Love

As my healing journey progressed post-hypnosis and through the early days of my trauma therapy—probably around the same time I could first identify my emotional needs—I realized I'd never received the love I needed from the three people I most expected to love me: my mom, my dad, and Tristan. Initially, this realization was devastating and heartbreaking, bringing deep sadness and despair. Some days, I was in mourning for my own deprivation and found it difficult to get out of bed and function. My inner critic became consumed with a million questions and cruel self-talk, fighting to keep me behind my wall.

Have I done something to make them not love me?

Have I behaved in a way that pushed them away from me?

Was I not good enough as a daughter or wife?

Do I deserve their love?

Do I know what love is?

Do I know how to receive love?

Do I know how to give love?

Can I be loved?

Am I lovable?

Can I even recognize the love I need?

While the question as to whether I was lovable was the scariest, the last question about whether I would recognize the love I needed was like a death knell. If I had never been loved this way, did I even know what it looked like? How can you know what you're looking for if you haven't experienced it? This was the turning point in my healing journey, wherein love became front and center in my focus.

As my exploration began, the first place I saw love was with my friends Sally and Kate. The night they let me pour out to them when they received my words without judgment and offered back only compassion, understanding, and affirmation, was the first time I ever recognized something resembling real love. The incredulous and puzzled looks on their faces showed me they were trying to reconcile the *me* they had known with the *me* they were staring at. Me, with my all-put-together paint and veneer—juxtaposed with the devastated-and-wrecked me sharing what probably seemed like unbelievable tales of abuse and trauma. I will never forget how I felt that night. Bewildered, confused, and scared, but loved.

Although I didn't know it then, I now know, of course, that I felt this because they met 100 percent of my emotional needs for acceptance, unconditional love, and communication. They accepted what I said without any rebuttal or rejection. They loved me, still, despite what I told them about the events in my life, and they never asked me to change in any way. In fact, they wanted to know who I *really* was, and to do that, they knew I needed help. They could already see what I came to know as my wall. And they communicated with me in an honest and transparent way. They told me the good and the bad—honestly and from their hearts—and where to start my healing journey.

Finding this love through their friendship ignited my fire to know love more completely. As I continued my quest, I found love everywhere I looked. I found love in old friends who I hadn't spoken to in years, as I had alienated them as I retreated behind my wall. I found love in Natalie as I continued to pull her out of exile. I found love in some of my coworkers, including my boss and peers who technically reported to me, as well as in other business acquaintances with whom I shared my story. All these people accepted what I said about myself with unconditional love.

Interestingly—but it's probably no surprise when I say this—those people who I now feel the deepest sense of reciprocal love with are part of my support team. I rely on them to help me through the hard times and to celebrate my successes. They are the truest loves of my life because what I receive from them sustains my heart. I hope I give back to them in the same way.

My quest for love eventually led me to seek intimate love with a man as my life partner. For a fleeting moment, I found that love in John. He gave me the sweetest taste of what it feels like to be loved in the way I need. He listened to me through difficult conversations wherein I shared things about myself I had never told anyone else. He didn't reject any part of me, and he didn't ask me to be anything other than who I am. He also encouraged me to always seek my best self.

But through our relationship, I learned one of my toughest lessons yet about being a survivor. His choice to live as an alcoholic rather than do his own work to overcome his addiction is why my taste of this love only lasted for a fleeting moment. He was quite ill, could not control his affliction, and refused to get help.

I struggled to understand why someone who loved me so deeply and had helped me grow to see the beautiful person I was couldn't love himself enough to get healthy—for himself first and then for us. I had many *why* questions to the Universe…including *Why would the Universe allow me to choose him, getting such a short-lived taste of the love I needed?*

Ultimately, I came to understand that John may have only been in my life to teach me and to help me progress in my search to know love. He gave me that sweet taste of this source of love so that I could know what I was looking for. He also solidified my understanding that if someone isn't ready to heal, they won't.

The greatest lesson I learned from John, however, had been missing from my quest. It's crazy because it's the source where love truly begins. That source is *self-love*. Ironically, I discovered that because of my self-love, I'm the one who couldn't love him unconditionally and accept him for exactly who he was. His behavior was destructive for both of us, and I refused to continue to live in trauma. Despite how I felt about him, I walked away. And under similar circumstances, I would do it again. I would do it for myself because I love myself and my inner peace more than anyone or anything else.

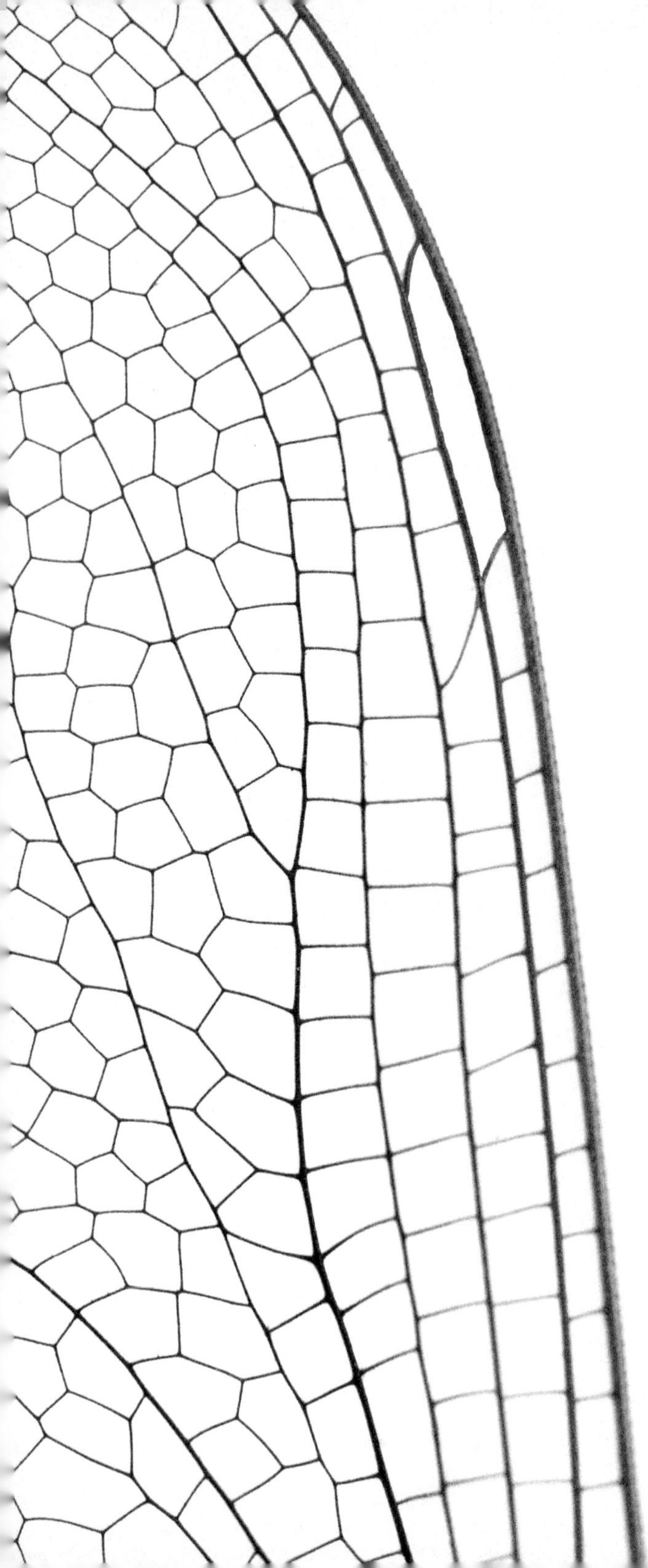

CHAPTER 10

FOSTERING SELF-LOVE

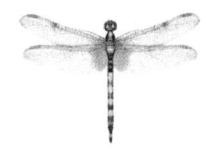

SELF-LOVE ALSO SEEMS to bring misconceptions, including for me. I learned the hard way what it means. It's so simple, really, yet it can be so difficult for us, as survivors, to understand.

Eventually, it was my struggle with John that brought me to my awakening. Touched again by the Universe, I realized the only person who could *truly* love *me* as I need to be loved is me.

As the turmoil of our relationship escalated, I spent a lot of time moving outside in nature. As I moved, I processed my emotions and thoughts about our relationship through the rhythmic motion of my body, mimicking the EMDR in my trauma therapy.

One day, after months of escalating turmoil in our relationship, my frustration erupted over the situation and with myself because I was still being reactionary in an unhealthy way—including with my anger. During my walk that day, I was deep in my familiar rhythmic state, but my processing was next-level compared to most days. Highly emotional, which was probably evident to any passerby, I kicked at whatever lay on the ground before me. I stomped my feet and stood at street corners with clenched fists. Sometimes, my hands flew up in the air as I questioned the Universe about so many things in our relationship. Marginally aware of my surroundings, I didn't care.

I intensely discussed the situation with myself, focusing all of my questions on our relationship and what it had become, who he was, and why he couldn't do what I needed him to do—heal—for us. My mind reeled with anger, my heart deep in sadness. I was grieving the end of our relationship.

But I was entirely focused on him or us.

Suddenly, out of nowhere, the Universe touched me with a soft hand and gently turned my attention toward myself. It was as if the Universe, my guardian angel, reached down and removed all of my thoughts of *him and us* so that I could see *me*. Just me and the sufficiency of who I was to sustain my own love and meet my emotional needs. I knew at that moment that I had inside of me all that I was looking for from a loving partner. I also knew I was the only person who *truly* knew who I was and what I needed to be emotionally fulfilled.

Though I'm still working at it, by then, I had done a lot of work to accept myself as the complete person I was, with the capacity to love myself unconditionally. Indeed, my commitment and desire to heal are rooted in my love for myself. And loving myself unconditionally now means I choose actions for my highest and best good, ruling myself with my head rather than my heart during difficult decisions.

Loving myself means accepting everything I've learned about myself through my evolution. I am the person for whom I have the most grace. Loving myself means accepting my vulnerabilities and limitations, as well as my strengths and gifts. Loving myself means that although I occasionally hear my inner critic, today, I can gently love her and ask her to be a little quieter than she used to be.

Now I know that all I need has always been inside of me. True love is self-love. No one can love me or you better than we can love ourselves. Today, I know I'm enough. I also know that you're enough.

My mantra, "self-love first," is a positive affirmation I use daily to remind myself of how important self-love is to my overall well-being.

In the wise words of the indomitable Ru Paul, uttered as each episode of the reality TV show *Drag Race* ends: "If you can't love yourself, how the hell you gonna love somebody else?"

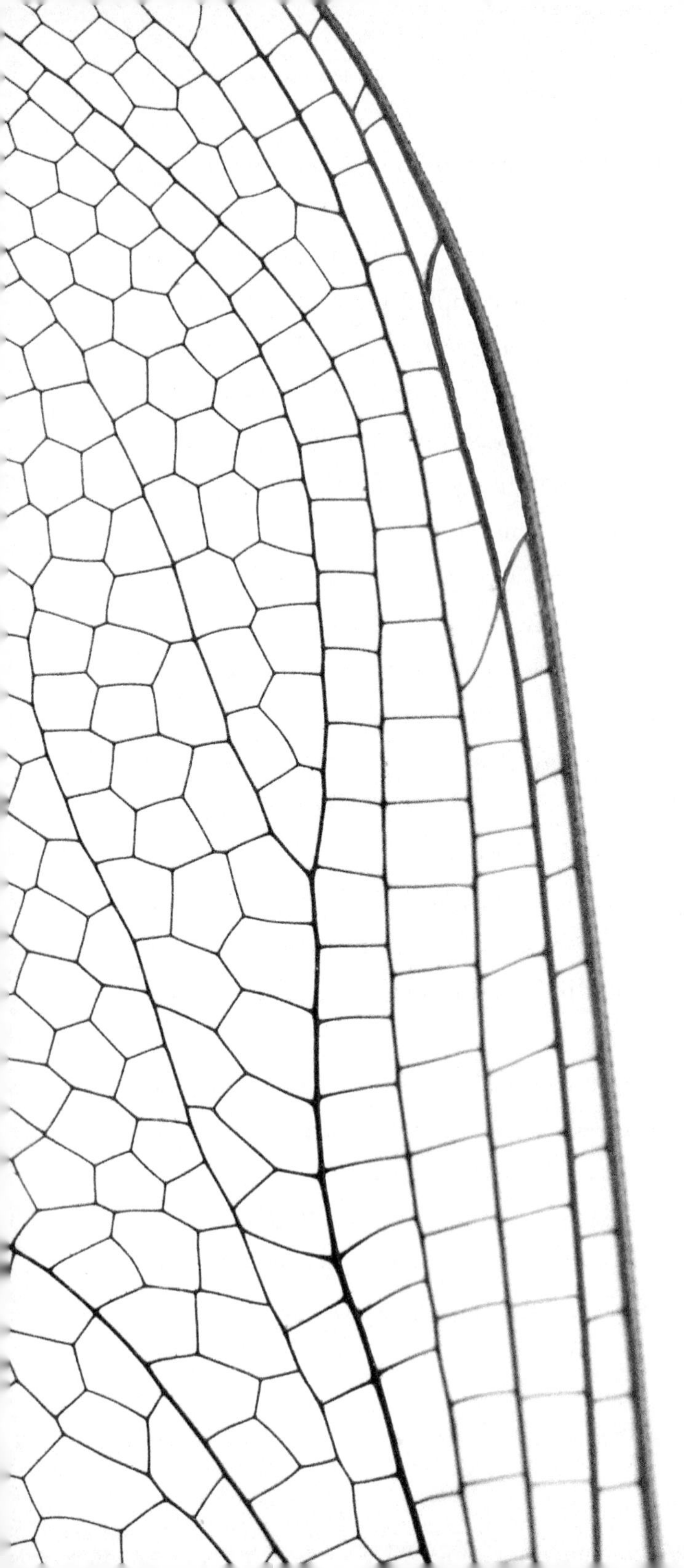

CHAPTER 11

ADDRESSING HURTFUL RELATIONSHIPS

Even though my healing work brought grace for and acceptance of the people who hurt me, I still had to address my continued participation in each relationship. A relationship didn't change just because I'd done the work to see them as a survivor reflected in me. Rather, I needed to take action to stop the other person from hurting me. When another person is still living encumbered by their own unhealthy survivorship, this is even more crucial to our healing process.

In this situation, I found three choices:

1. Continue the relationship as is,
2. End the relationship, or
3. Continue the relationship but in a new way.

Choosing between these is a matter that involves both heart and head. My heart feels what it feels and longs for what it longs for. As an eternal optimist, I'm hopeful for the other person. But this is where the flip side of my hope can have a sharp edge. Sometimes, my hope causes me to hang on far too long, hoping for a change, a different outcome that most likely will never come. This is where my head steps in and evaluates the other person—their words *and* actions—to determine whether I think the relationship can continue in the right way for me.

In the past, these relationships profoundly impacted and defined my life. I struggled to make decisions because matters of the heart can be complicated. My gut instinct and spirituality ultimately weighed heavily in my decisions.

I've discovered two crucial tenets to making choices in a relationship. First, my decision must be based on what's right for me and my highest and best good. In other words, *self-love first*. I've already talked about this tenet. The second tenet is that I make better decisions when I act from a more healed place with respect to myself and the relationship. I make better decisions after I've mirrored and seen the other person as a human being who is suffering, just like me. I don't want to create a long-term, and perhaps permanent, impact from a place of unhealthy emotion.

I don't want to react in the moment out of anger and cause permanent damage. Otherwise, I may get a final outcome that's not in my best interest. Or I may hurt the other person, which isn't my intention. My decision is not about revenge or punishment.

I've also found it beneficial to my loving spirit to try and see the good in the relationship, including my lessons learned, and to have genuine gratitude for this learning. This extends the grace and acceptance from mirroring, helping me see what the Universe sought to teach me through the relationship. At this point, the relationship becomes about me and understanding the benefits, and not about them and how they hurt me.

I'm going to give you examples of how I made each of these decisions—continue as is, end the relationship, or continue in a new way—within some of my most significant relationships. In some cases, I've made more than one decision over the course of the relationship, which is another truth about surviving and healing. When we're actively surviving a relationship, we continue as is, waiting until we're healed enough to do something different.

As the saying goes, "If nothing changes, nothing changes. If you keep doing what you're doing, you're going to keep getting what you're getting. You want change, make some" (Courtney C. Stevens, *The Lies About Truth*). This is simple but profound and so very accurate. Change is inevitable if you want to live your highest and best good.

Continue the Relationship as Is

For most of those years Tristan and I were married, I chose to continue our relationship as is. I had no idea that I needed to make changes in my relationship. Until my time came to heal, I never saw the point at which the relationship ceased serving me. Instead, I just sat in it.

Even as I began to realize the relationship wasn't serving me, which probably happened more than ten years before I ended it, I chose to continue as is. I made that choice from a place of survival and just trying to get through every day. I wasn't healed or healing, so I couldn't make a better decision for myself.

Many of us choose, unwittingly, to stay in a relationship with an unhealthy person. We don't know that we need to make a change, or perhaps we don't dare to put ourselves first. So we don't do what we know we should. We don't realize we must choose self-love.

End the Relationship

I chose to end my marriage once I understood two things. First, I realized continuing our relationship was no longer possible for many reasons. Second, I saw that Tristan, by his own admission, wasn't going to work sufficiently to heal from his unhealthy survivorship, which impacted me negatively. He wasn't going to evolve the way I needed in order for me to stay. I accepted what my inner knowing, my head, told me.

I also believe he was ill-equipped to help me. He didn't know how to help me. I didn't know how to help myself! As we fought during the day, I discovered my emotional needs; I knew definitively that our marriage wasn't going to survive who I was becoming. I knew the evolved me would be a very different person. And I knew he could no longer serve my highest and best good.

I begged him to join me in walking his own healing journey so we could evolve together and perhaps save our relationship. But he wouldn't do it. "You're a fast-moving train speeding away from the depot. I see you getting further and further away, and I can't keep up," he said that day. That made me angry at the time, and I thought it was a copout.

For years before, he had done much of his work to try to heal. The modalities he used mostly involved meeting and trying to vanquish his demons in the spirit world. Revealed under a shamanic journey or using ayahuasca, these demons were those people in his life who hurt him. (You can research more on this, but ayahuasca is a psychoactive brew made from certain plants, traditionally used by indigenous people in South America for spiritual ceremonies and healing.) But he wasn't getting educated about what we were both suffering from and how it impacted us. He was in individual therapy, and we tried couple's therapy one last time, but my guess is his individual therapy was more akin to just sitting on the couch. That certainly was true for the couple's therapy. He wasn't willing to jump on the train with me, so in the end, I left the train depot for good.

Like me, he, too, was a spiritual person. Shortly after he arrived in Thailand, he had his own premonition about what was to come. One morning, he sent me a photo of his breakfast guest and told me about their encounter that day. He was seated beside a floor-to-ceiling plate-glass window, and on the lower windowsill, he saw a dragonfly resting. Apparently, it was trapped in the room, struggling with the windows, but it had settled beside him to rest. Because Tristan could never stand by and watch any animal struggle or suffer, he found a way to free the insect. Only a few months later, he said to me, the day he acknowledged we should part ways, "It's time for me to set you free." Me and my dragonfly spirit. "Fly high, dragonfly," he said to me a couple of times, encouragingly, after that day.

We went through six months of settlement negotiations to separate our lives—mostly our finances and possessions, because we didn't have children. He had his dog with him. I had *our* dog—who moved to the Philippines with my friend when I left Hong Kong—and my cat. Although I knew I had to leave the relationship, it took this time to get to the point where he would finally let me go. During that time, I fought hard not to harbor any feelings of anger, or worse, hatred, toward him. I didn't want those feelings, such that the relationship would continue to hold bondage over me.

Sally and Kate showed me a lot of love during those months. One day, Sally called me right after Tristan and I argued. I don't recall what this fight was about—there were a lot during these months of working out our separation—but

I was very angry and in despair after it ended. As soon as I heard her voice, I began to pour out my anger, not at her, but toward her. And an astonishing thing happened. She took my anger away from me. It was as if I transferred my anger to her, and because she had no vested interest, she could hold it for a little bit, be angry on my behalf, and then let it go. I was and am still amazed at how easy that was. I was able to share what I felt with someone who cared very much about my well-being, and my sharing became a transfer. I've since experienced this phenomenon several times with Sally and Kate. They've been angry with me, and they've been sad for me. And then I've been okay because those feelings didn't linger inside of me.

As easily as they give me joy, so, too, do they willingly take my anger and sadness. This is one of the greatest expressions of their love for me. It's also a strong testament to having the right support team and not being afraid to be authentic and open with them.

Working through my emotions over Tristan was the next time after dealing with my grandfather that I practiced mirroring, and it's probably when I began to realize its power to help me let go. Tristan's actions had never been about being abusive, controlling, or domineering over me. Rather, he lived with unhealthy survivorship, just like I did.

I was letting go during those months, and I wanted to find gratitude for him and our relationship. Not all the thirty-plus years we shared were bad. In fact, we had many good years and some good times during the difficult years.

He taught me a lot, including about surviving. This included not only abuse and trauma survivorship but also skills that extended my independence, like how to survive more than a few days without electricity and central heat during a major snowstorm. He taught me to drive a manual transmission on an old 1950s Massey-Ferguson tractor. And he taught me the exhilaration of running through the gears of a race car.

We also learned a lot together, like how to operate a working ranch. If you know what those two words mean, "working ranch," then you know how much we learned. Completely learned behavior for me. We had a lot of joy with our animals, especially puppies, kittens, calves, goat kids, and foals. I found plenty to be grateful for, and I felt it was (is) important to hold onto those memories, even though I was letting go.

During the months it took to reach a settlement, I often practiced gratitude for him. Some days, it was part of my quiet meditation time. Other days, it was a way of processing what was happening to us. And other days, it was a way of offsetting my anger at him, particularly if I hadn't been able to transfer that feeling to Sally or Kate.

I'm unsure when I began looking for the lessons I had been taught in my marriage, particularly about my behavior in our relationship and what I wanted (or didn't want) from an intimate relationship with my partner. This evolved over time as I worked to release the extreme ends of my feelings for Tristan. Love and hate, or jubilation and anger, were replaced with only caring about the well-being of someone once significant in my life but for whom I no longer held an emotional connection.

I now have compassion and empathy for Tristan as a human being and as a survivor, but my emotions of intimacy are gone. Today, I only have neutral emotions and peace toward the relationship, even when his actions occasionally provoke a fleeting moment of frustration. I am human, and he still is who he is. Neutrality is how I know the relationship is healed for me. Indeed, this may be one of my biggest lessons yet. I've learned from my healing work around my marriage that I know I'm truly done with a relationship when I can let it go.

Many of my self-evolution lessons were instilled during and because of my marriage. These lessons have shaped my expectations for the future man in my life who will be lucky to have me in his. I couldn't love today had I not experienced this relationship with Tristan as it was. For this, I'm truly grateful for him and for our marriage.

With John, I made the same decision to end our relationship for the same reasons and using the same process. That was a harder decision, given my quest to know love. The hardest part was that the good was so good at first that after I tasted it, I craved it and feared I would never find it again.

But as he continued to hurt me, I inched further away from him. Each time, my hope for a better future shattered just a little bit more. *Maybe this is the time*, I would tell myself. But that time never came.

One day, reacting rather than responding to some harsh and hurtful words he lobbed my way—including calling me a "victim," but in a misplaced and derogatory way—I decided to cut all ties, blocking him in every possible communication modality. The next day, I had a heart-versus-head battle. My heart longed for the good parts of our relationship, but my head knew I was never going to have that again. I knew I must dig deep into myself and find the will to resist him. Literally, I pulled on my strength and willpower not to reconnect with him in any way. It was like resisting the urge for just one more cigarette or just one more drink. Even one moment of contact, and I would have been trapped in the ongoing cycle of going nowhere. I agonized about my battle with Monica. "Why can't I just let go?" I pleaded to her.

But then, one day, after drawing my strength from deep inside (and having no contact), I did just that. I simply let go.

Continue the Relationship in a New Way

My story about my relationship with my parents is one of my most powerful tales about the beauty found in healing. I've known for a while now that it must be told publicly. The opportunity to share this story with other survivors is one of the reasons I wrote this book. I've come full circle in my relationship with my parents, and it is a magnificent circle.

My exile of my parents lasted for more than ten years. When I ended our relationship, I felt I had no choice. I felt emotionally unsafe when I talked to or fought with my mom. As our interactions escalated in intensity, my dad was physically absent for much of the time because he worked offshore, twenty-eight-plus days away in Kazakhstan, and only about three and a half weeks stateside between each rotation. When he was stateside, he rarely contacted me. When he did, I felt him guilt-tripping me about not checking on my mom when he was gone. He was worried about her well-being, telling me once, "She could die by herself alone, and no one would know or care." He never asked to understand my *why* or my feelings. *Unacknowledged* is a good word for how I felt about my dad toward my feelings.

My parents and Tristan never liked each other, and trapping me in the middle only complicated my situation. Ironically, I think one of their reasons for this was a desire to protect me from the other. In the end, I chose to align with Tristan's wishes. In fact, I exiled my parents under the heavy influence of his "them or me" ultimatum.

Having said that, to be fair, I was the one who chose to end our relationship. I decided I needed to remove myself from the awful place our relationship was in. The only way I could see to break away from the constant feed of this chaos and drama (I dreaded holidays for many years) was to step out of the relationship.

I got the relief I needed, but I suffered two major consequences. The first was that I no longer had my parents in my life, and I believed there was almost no chance we would ever repair our relationship. In fact, one of the issues I dealt with during those years of unsuccessful therapy was whether I had *really* accepted losing them. The question of how I would feel if they were to die always came up. I avoided answering and told my therapist with a stern face, "Oh, I'll be fine, totally fine."

"Frustrated, Insecure, Neurotic, and Emotional" is how my mom defines the word *fine*. She would have been correct had the dreadful occurred.

During those years, I worked hard to ensure people didn't interpret my estrangement as something I had done wrong. Remember, I didn't have the vocabulary of a survivor back then. I didn't yet have the word *parentectomy*, so I engaged in a contorted explanation of why we no longer had a relationship. I wasn't embarrassed about the state of our relationship, but I didn't want anyone to think it was my fault because of some awful thing I did.

The other consequence of exiling my parents was my *familyectomy*.

Reclaiming my relationship with my parents began with Natalie. For about two years before I began my post-hypnotherapy relationship reclamation work, we communicated off and on, but we talked mainly about events in her life. She initiated our original reconnect, and I didn't know at the time that she was also looking for that same true love I was seeking. She wanted me to become part of her support team. She was looking for the same qualities I would later look for: partnership and love. I gave her what she needed when she needed me.

That night I ended my exile of her came through pure serendipity. I happened to be in Dallas for a business trip (my largest project in Hong Kong often brought me to Dallas since it held the US headquarters for the Chinese company I worked for). Somehow, she found out I was coming in and took a chance to ask me to dinner, not knowing how I would respond. I saw her for the first time in a long time at about 5 p.m. that evening. Just before midnight, we were nudged to pay our bill. Our time together had flown by like lightning, but we were radiating love for each other. Even the waitstaff could feel it.

"Yes, we're sisters. This is the first time we've seen each other in a long time," we explained.

"Wow! You seem so at ease with each other and like you always do this!"

We closed the restaurant and never looked back from that night. But it took what I was going through two years later to boost the regularity of our communication and the mainstay nature of our relationship.

Natalie was one of my biggest supporters as I described what happened during my hypnotherapy—including how I felt, what I learned, and my decision to end my marriage. We talked a lot during the early months, post-hypnotherapy, about our childhoods growing up outside of the US and some about our family, including our grandfather. We found our experiences growing up were very different. We're almost nine years apart, and because of our age difference, the first half of my childhood and the second half of hers were spent as only children. There wasn't much day-to-day commonality in the environment we grew up in; she was too young when our years under the same roof overlapped.

We could have chosen to live our adult lives in the same way. But we chose to continue our relationship in a new way, though we needed few boundaries. We now have an understanding as sisters that no one else can have. We're sisters by blood, but we're fierce supporters by choice.

Eventually, our conversations turned to our parents. Natalie had always remained close to them, and while she was respectful of my privacy, she told them some of the things happening to me. She shared about my life-altering event, that I was going through a serious healing process, and that I was working on reclaiming important relationships.

At the same time, I was talking to John about my relationship with my parents. He accepted my reasons for the exile but encouraged me to consider reconciling. His work with me toward reclaiming my relationship with them is one of the amazingly good things I got from our relationship; I will always be grateful for this.

I made my first pandemic-era visit to the US from Hong Kong in the summer of 2021 about fourteen months after my hypnotherapy. I was stuck in Hong Kong because of their strict control measures, which essentially shut the city's borders entirely to the outside world, trapping the residents within. A mandatory three-week quarantine in a hotel (at the traveler's expense) upon return from just about any part of the world, including the US, meant that leaving Hong Kong wasn't an easy decision. Also, some other rigid and complicated logistical arrangements that accompanied the exit and reentry meant everything had to be planned and executed *perfectly.* For example, a quarantine reservation had to begin within a few hours of your flight arriving in Hong Kong. Flight delays posed a real and significant risk. And mother nature can't be controlled.

For about four months before I made the trip, my conversations with Monica, Natalie, and John about the situation with my parents escalated in frequency and seriousness. I could feel an intensifying urge to try to reclaim the relationship building inside of me, but I was still so hesitant.

A couple of months before my trip, I sent my mom a text message. For years by then, in the rare instance when we did communicate, it was by text. I don't recall whether I heard my mom's voice in all those years. I doubt it.

I told her I was coming to Texas for a visit and that I might want to reconnect, but I had two criteria. The first was that my parents had to accept whatever I told them factually about me, including the abuse I suffered. Facts are facts—the truth—and I needed them to accept those things without any resistance or rejection. The generational, familial abuse had been a taboo subject for all my life, and the flat rejection of facts had escalated when my aunt told her daughters what she experienced. My parent's rejection, my dad's especially, extended to anyone who even hinted at having the same experience. Perhaps this is part of why my own memories and acceptance of what happened to me were suppressed for so many years. A family unconsciousness.

My second criterion was that our interactions had to be peaceful. I wanted no part of the drama, chaos, or fighting that had consumed my past relationship with my mom. My life had been more peaceful for many years by then, especially since I had been living in Hong Kong, and I wasn't willing to give up my serenity.

With those two criteria, I began to set my boundaries and work to continue our relationship in a new way. I was expressing my needs in the relationship to protect myself, acting out of self-love, and defining the key parameters by which I would engage with my parents. I was putting myself forward in a new way to see whether we could repair our relationship.

Will they meet me halfway? I hoped.

When I sent the message, I was afraid and filled with angst. I wondered what my mom's response would be, if she responded at all. For days thereafter, every morning when I woke up in Hong Kong, I first checked my messages, looking for any response she might have sent during her day. Seven weeks passed without a response.

Each passing day was more agonizing and disappointing than the previous. I was devastated and confused because I had been sure the Universe was paving the way for me to reclaim our relationship. I was healed enough by then to try. *You've led me to this place, God. Why isn't she responding?*

Then, the Universe touched me again through another mirroring experience. Although I knew both of my parents were survivors who coped in their own ways, perhaps they still were. I realized her lack of response might be her own boundary to protect herself, just like I was doing. My estrangement had caused my parents a lot of pain, so I could understand that she, too, may have been shielding herself, my dad, and their hearts. And so began my process to accept that our relationship might be dead.

I don't know whether it was my acceptance of why my mom may not have responded, my acceptance of my parents as survivors, and/or my acceptance that *I* had made the decision to exile them, but I came to a point where I had grace for and acceptance of them. I recalled the parts that had been so good while growing up—not the least of which was my international upbringing, which profoundly impacted who I became. I found gratitude for all the gifts from my life with them. They instilled in me strong ethics and values, and they gave me an education. Both provided me with my career and financial security. I suppose, in a way, I mourned the loss of our relationship during my exile. But now I also know I was preparing to accept the finality of our relationship if finality came.

And then, one morning, one week before my trip, a message came. My heart raced with anticipation as I eagerly, but with trepidation, read her reply. I would like to tell you that her response made me leap with joy—the feeling you might have if the sky was filled with sunshine and rainbows over a field of spring tulips with bluebirds chirping happily and puppies running around in play.... You get the idea.

That's not how I felt. Not even close.

"We'll see about doing that. When will you be here?" were the only words in that message.

I was anticipating something more positive and reassuring, something that would have made me feel like she was trying to understand me, embrace me, and commit to whatever it would take to bring us back together. I was let down and deflated after my building anticipation and anxiety over the preceding weeks. But it was a response and a response wherein I understood she knew the expectations and meaning behind my two criteria. Only time would tell whether she—they—would be able to respect my boundaries.

It took me eight of my ten weeks in the US on that trip to get the courage to call my mom. I didn't want to see her. A voice call was all I had planned for. It took me that long because her response to my message had been so noncommittal, almost flippant, and I was scared that I was risking disappointment and heartbreak if I just got more of what I remembered from our interactions before their exile. I wondered, *What if she is the exact same person as she was back then?*

My mom knew I was stateside, and she kept calling my sister. The urgency increased as my trip drew to an end. "Do you know why Beth isn't calling me?" Mom kept asking.

Natalie had always been good about refraining from being the peacemaker between us, respecting the needs of both my parents and me as we worked through our relationship, including during the years of our estrangement. But with increasing frequency, almost to the point of being frantic, my mom pestered Natalie for information about whether I was still in the US. Mom was eager to talk to me for the same reasons I wanted to talk to her: to see whether we could reclaim our relationship.

At the same time, John increasingly encouraged me to call my mom. One day, the topic of my mom dominated my conversations with both Natalie and him. The weight of both conversations was my final sign. *The time has come,* I told myself that night in bed. *Tomorrow will be the day.*

I was nervous when I called her the next morning. I felt like it might be my last chance to see what was possible. I thought about our history and how we had arrived at that place in our relationship. I reaffirmed my reasons for exiling them. I thought about my healing journey and how it had guided me every step of the way to that point, without fail, through a transformational process. I thought about the success I'd had in reclaiming my relationships with my sister and my friends. And I trusted I was exactly where the Universe meant for me to be that morning before I made the call.

I'm not sure why—perhaps it was the Universe intervening this time—but I chose a video call. She answered immediately. It startled me when I saw her because she had fully embraced the aging process with a full head of gray hair. I gasped, not expecting to see that. Rather, I had expected to see the woman I'd last seen in person some ten years earlier, after which I saw pictures of her from time to time—like from my parent's fiftieth wedding anniversary celebration, which I missed, where she was still blonde. Even at her age, it never occurred to me that she might have decided to let her beautiful, silver-gray hair shine.

Seeing her stark hair change reminded me of the precious nature of our remaining time. In that instant, I knew this call was my one chance to move us in a direction to take advantage of that time before they were physically gone. My parents were in their mid-seventies by then, and although neither had any terminal illness, they were aging.

I called my mom at 9 a.m. She answered on the first ring.

"Hi, Mom," I offered.

"Hi, honey. Oh, thank goodness! I'm so glad you called. I was afraid you'd leave before we could talk."

Dull, idle chitchat...about the hot summer weather in Texas...then...

"This is weird for me, Mom. I don't even know where to start. I've been doing a lot of work to heal from some things I need for you to understand about me. My life has changed so radically. I really want to see whether we can have a relationship again."

"So do I. So does your dad. Tell me what's been happening to you. I just want to listen."

I could sense that something about her had changed.

"Your hair, Mom, is beautiful. Not what I expected to see. Not who I expected, but maybe it has a deeper meaning."

It was noon before I looked at the time again. I couldn't believe we had talked, just talked, for three hours. The time passed so fast, and it was a wonderful conversation. The perfect conversation.

That day, we weren't mother and daughter; rather, we talked as two people who had always been surviving—and were still trying to survive—our lives. We both accepted what the other said about our experiences, including how those events made us feel, how we responded—well or not so well—and sometimes why we responded as we had. Our conversation had no chaos or drama; it was calm and peaceful. She met both of my criteria.

We probably could have continued to talk for another three hours, but I had to go. We agreed to meet a few days later, just before I returned to Hong Kong. That, too, was another wonderful meeting and a step in the direction of reclaiming my relationship with my parents.

One of the reasons for my trip back to the US had been to consider an opportunity my company offered me. You could have knocked me over with a feather the day I was offered about three weeks before I visited Dallas. It didn't involve returning just to the US or even Texas but to Dallas—the big city that was the nucleus of where all my immediate and extended family lived. (Van is just ninety miles east of Dallas.) This opportunity to return came out of the blue. I couldn't believe the words I heard, despite my acute awareness by then that I was walking an intentional and focused journey that continued to open before me. The Universe was touching me again.

Seeing my mom was one of my final considerations in deciding to return. During my weeks in Dallas, I also spent time with Natalie and realized how much I missed her and wanted to *really* have her in my life, closer than a video call allowed. I now felt the same way about my parents, although

I wouldn't see my dad for another three months. So, I made the decision to move back permanently, mainly so I could continue reclaiming my relationship with my family.

And that's exactly what happened. I've been back for nearly three years now, and we've spent the time together as if the previous fifty years didn't happen as they did. We've acted like a family who truly loves each other. We all seem to have the same grace for and acceptance of one another as we each work on letting go of the hurtful parts of our past relationships. While there is some holding onto the past, which I think is normal for a family of survivors healing together, we can talk about it when the time is right, which seems to be for the purpose of helping us all heal. We're continuing our relationship but in a new way.

I also gained the gift of a relationship with my nephew and nieces, who have needs of their own, also as survivors. I have the privilege of helping them with their journeys. It's as if a wave of healing has been rolling over our entire family—and it's a big, rolling barrel wave of HEAL!

Exiling my family contributed significantly to my isolation behind my wall. While I know my reasons for doing this, and I felt at the time that I had no other option, now I can see this was self-inflicted harm. Similar to allowing our inner critic to be loud, this is a great example of the harm we can do to ourselves as survivors. I'm grateful daily for the profound impact of my healing work, which allowed me to repair these relationships.

I could tell you what I didn't do to help the relationship or avoid the separation from my parents, but that would only be me criticizing myself for something that wouldn't have been possible back then. The reality is that I wasn't ready to heal at that time, nor did I know how to. I needed to gain access to my tools—on my specific path—to heal. It wasn't my time to heal back then.

I also know I had to experience this event, including the loss of my family, as part of my purpose. Indeed, I couldn't share this beautiful story with you as a demonstration of the power of healing had I not exiled them and then done the work that allowed me to repair our relationship. I got my family back!

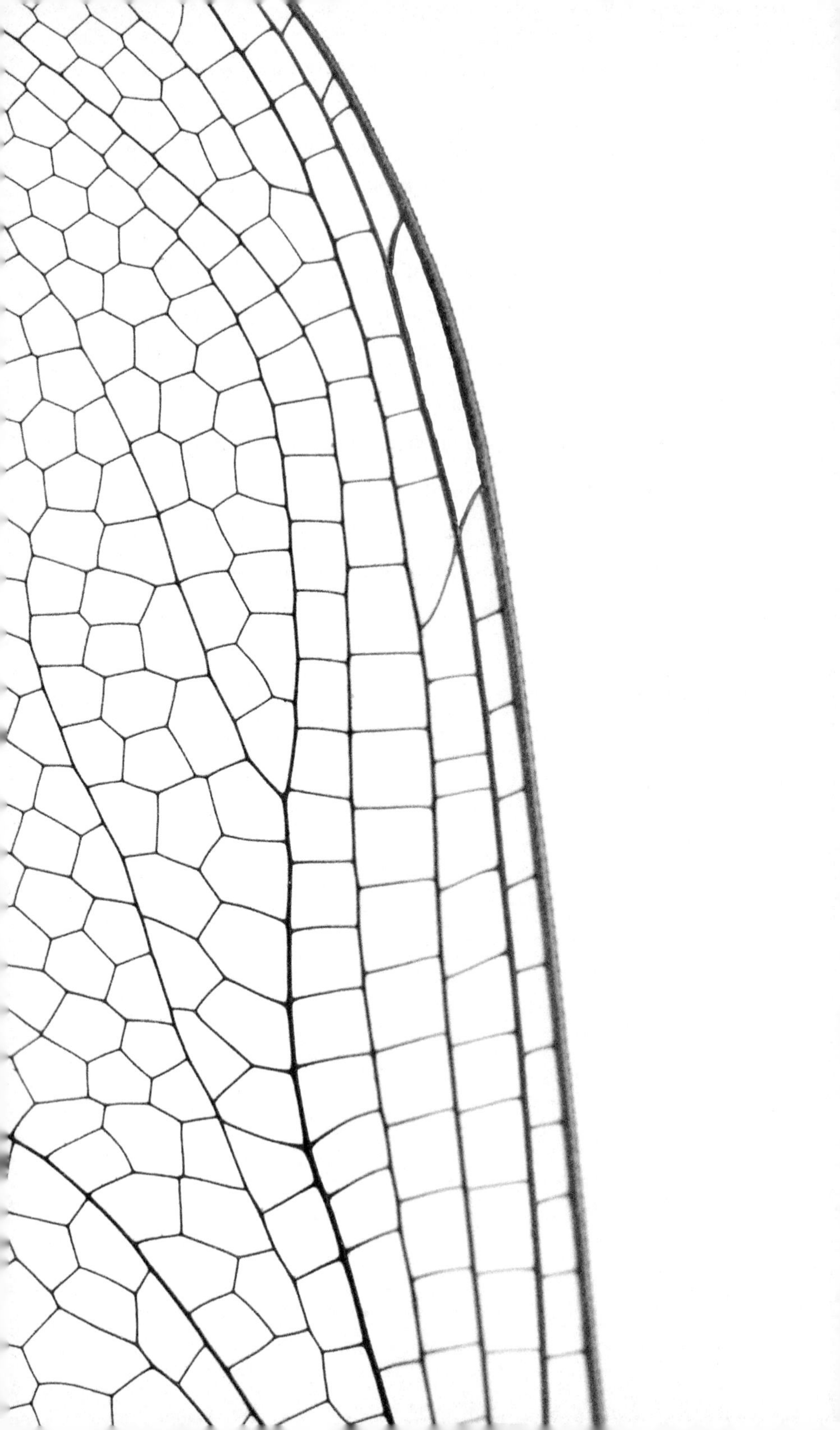

CHAPTER 12

EMBRACING HEALTHY RELATIONSHIPS

I BEGAN EXPLORING love through healthy relationships with people who had never hurt me. In this way, I received much of the love I needed, getting my emotional needs met in part or whole. These relationships also taught me how to give back so our love could be mutually nurtured then and into the future.

I didn't wake up one day and suddenly know love. Instead, I explored and am still exploring it with intention and focus on getting it right for myself. Feeding my emotional needs is at the core of feeling loved. Healthy, genuinely loving relationships should be symbiotic.

Often, this can be experienced in a friendship. As I said before, I first noticed myself experiencing love and emotional nurturing in my relationship with Sally and Kate. My relationship with my friend Farrah is another excellent example of the symbiosis of reciprocal love. She is one of my oldest friends and has always given me acceptance and unconditional love, no matter what. We met in college and were pledge sisters in our fraternity. We became very close, even living together for a period, and our bond ever since has transcended time, including the years I lived behind my wall, disconnected from her. She was with me from the beginning of my journey to become "an American," in those years when I did simple things like learn how to boil water and make macaroni and cheese. And she was with me throughout my relationships with Tristan and John. We all knew each other in college.

No matter what I've done, Farrah has always been there for me—even when I blocked her on the outside of my wall for so many years. I can tell her anything, and she never judges me. But she will give me her opinion and advice, telling me when she thinks I'm doing something I need to rethink. I'm blessed that Farrah is one of the people I've been able to reclaim a friendship with. My work to bring her back to my support team began during those early months of the intentional and focused part of my healing journey. She was one of the first people from my past to whom I opened my heart. When I did, her heart met mine with a warm embrace as if no time had passed. She listened to everything I told her, accepting me with the unconditional love I always felt from her.

She lives near Dallas, which is another blessing of being back in this city, so we often see each other. As we have spent time together traveling in my journey, she is more than just a friend. We have interconnected souls. She has been through a long and traumatic relationship with someone who is very much like John. Their behaviors—including severe alcoholism—track almost in parallel, and she can tell me what is coming long before it happens. In this way, I was more prepared for whatever happened to him, which lessened the blow's severity for me.

She also kept me grounded in the reality of the likely eventual outcome of my relationship—and my decision to end it. She knew the best thing for me was to choose self-love. She did the same for herself, choosing herself and her health over someone she loved—showing me how to do it through her actions. She also stood by me as I agonized over my decision, sometimes speaking frustration with me when I prolonged my inevitable best outcome. But she never told me what to do. She let me find my own way and never abandoned me.

Farrah's person is no longer living on this Earth. Because of her, I, too, am a little bit prepared should that outcome ever happen in my life.

At least in a small way, Farrah's experiences happened to help me as I healed. Years ago, we forged a bond that transcended friendship, allowing us to come back together so easily when I needed her. Today, I know she has undoubtedly walked her path before me so that she can teach me and help me walk mine.

Farrah is one of the strongest and most resilient human beings I know. She is also quite happy being all by herself. Still, she, too, is looking to have people in her life who truly love her. She has lived through the ups and downs of relationships, and I'm blessed now to help her through some of her own challenges. She needs to talk about what she is experiencing and feeling without judgment. She, too, needs acceptance and unconditional love, which I can and do give her.

I have had other friendships wherein my giving to them was important to our reciprocal love. These friends experienced the worst parts of my relationship with Tristan when it took a turn long before it ended. In some cases, they still have a relationship with him today. As we divorced, a moment of pause allowed them to work out how to engage with me, given their ongoing relationship with him. As part of loving them—giving back to them—I hold no expectation that they choose sides. In fact, I've told them Tristan needs his own support team, and if they want to be a part of his life, I'm okay with that and encourage it.

I've also been reminded about friends who helped me during some of the worst chaos that I lived through—in Combine, for example—simply because they cared about me. Three men, in particular, helped to restore my faith in men, which was important given that men rendered most of the pain I'd experienced. One was the guy who helped clean up the damage to the property. Another was the guy for whom we owner-financed the property when he bought it from us. And the last was the lawyer who helped us battle with the city over our servals. He also helped us navigate with the real estate agent and inspector over every problem with the house that wasn't disclosed or was "missed" when we made the purchase. These men are three of the finest people whom I have had the good fortune to know, all of whom, at the time, restored my faith in the goodness and honesty of people, not just men. They all remain friends today who I would trust with my life.

My mentoring relationships at work have been some of my richest. These people are part of my support team because they allow me to do two things. First, they allow me to be authentic. There, achieving real inclusion—not asking any employee to leave a part of themselves outside the front door each day—is something I believe we still must work on in our organizations. Whether my mentor or my mentee, these people accept me for all of who I am, not just who they think I am or expect me to be.

Second, these relationships allow me to practice teaching as a healing mentor. For a while now, because I believe in inclusion and because building real relationships requires us to be authentic about who we are, I've been talking at work about my experiences. When I do this, people seek me out to connect, and they want to share. Because I talk openly, they talk openly. Because I'm unafraid of sharing my experiences and feelings, they are less afraid to share about themselves. I can help them to see it's okay to not be okay, even in the workplace.

These relationships have taught me the value I must pass on to others from my experiences, my healing journey, and how I think. I receive encouragement from them often to courageously continue my healing journey and pursue my work to help others heal. I can be myself. We share our experiences, and this allows me to step further into my life's purpose. In this way, we give and receive love.

Today, my support circle includes those who never hurt me: my sister, Natalie, lifelong and new friends, colleagues at work, mentors and mentees, and my trauma therapist, Monica. Someday, I hope I will be able to include a spouse or life partner (I'm working to get this one right!). Today, it also includes my parents because we are continuing our relationship in a new way. These people in my orbit truly care about me and contribute positively to my life by feeding my emotional needs. I'm healthy enough now that I won't settle for anything less, even if that means letting go of someone I love.

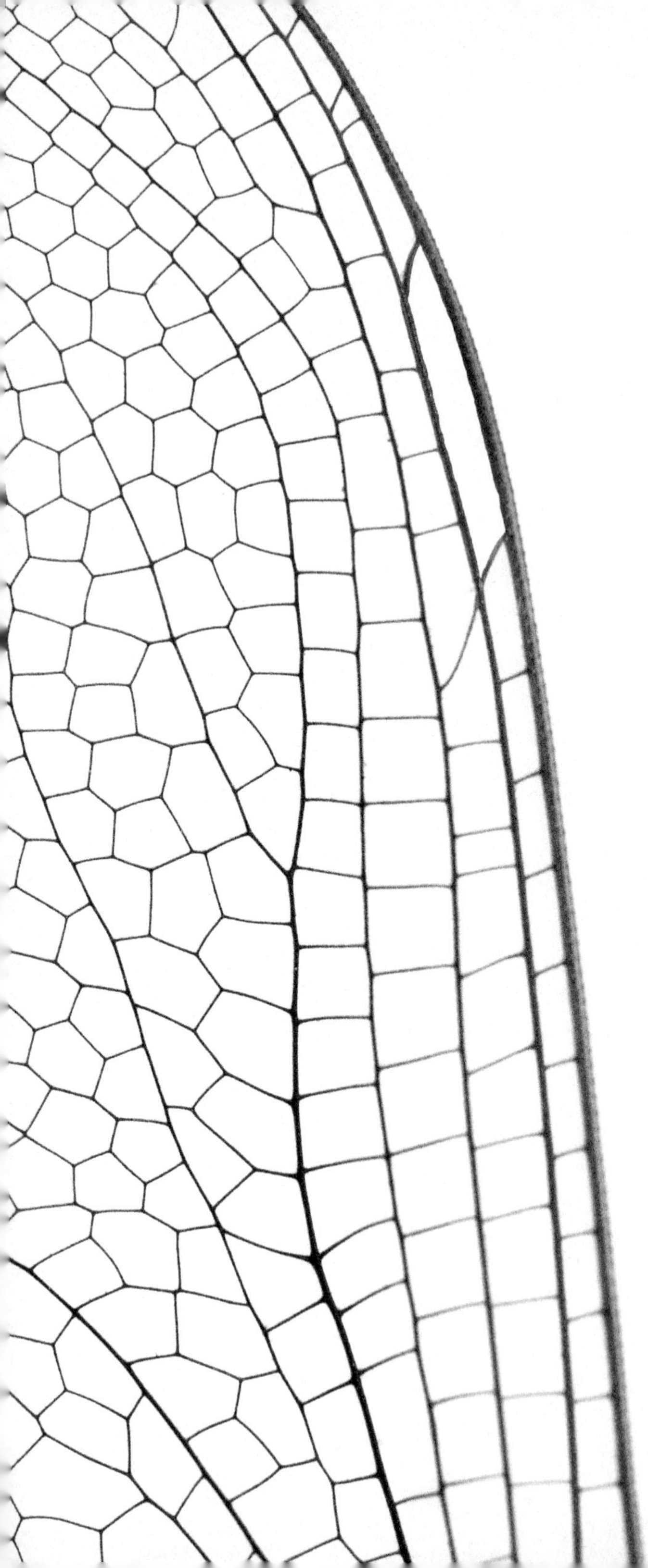

PART V
—
TOOLS TO HEAL

MOST ANYTHING WE create, build, or improve requires tools. Sometimes, our process can be difficult, so we may need different or more powerful tools to help us. Healing is no different. However, the tools we need individually and how we use them will vary for each of us.

In this section, I'll share the common tools that I've used, including my experience and how they've helped me. I'm doing this to help you think about how they might work for you and stimulate your thinking about other tools you already use. I hope you'll use some of my tools, perhaps differently from how I use them, and maybe add your own to your healing work.

Commitment

When my time to heal came, I knew it and set an intention and focus: I committed to walking my healing pathway, no matter where it led. In the blink of an eye, I recognized I was a victim and a survivor. I also saw my unhealthy survivorship built into my wall. Once I saw that, I literally shook my hands and thought, *Get this $*#@ off of me!*

Then, I committed to healing myself. Everything I've written in this book is about that commitment. And every decision that I've made, every day, big or small, has been about remaining steadfast.

If you want to heal, commit to yourself and be intentional about your work. Intentionally engage with your healing process. Make daily and long-term choices for your highest and best good. And focus on your end game: a life filled with true joy and love.

Books and Workbooks

For me, education often comes through reading books and using workbooks, which accompany many self-help books for survivors. Some books helped me see myself as a survivor and gave me a survivor's vocabulary. Others helped me recognize how we hurt each other from a place of unhealed survivorship. I saw other survivors healing. And some books helped me find my voice.

Some books deal with my own type of abuse—child sexual abuse, for example—which helped me understand what I experienced and the parts of my survivorship directly related to those events. These books also helped me to regain some vague memories of my childhood. They offered exercises intended to stimulate memories while avoiding triggering the worst of them. Following one book, for example, I tried an exercise to draw the floor plans of the bedrooms I lived in as a child. I still cannot remember it in any detail, but I did get certain memories that weren't a surprise to me, like the shade of pink or green in two of my bedrooms. I love color, so it's understandable that my memory held the hues vivid in my mind's eye.

Read if you want to get educated about what's happening to you as a survivor. Read if you want to understand trauma, survivorship, and overcoming the unhealthy ways in which we cope. Read if you want comfort or inspiration from other people who healed. And if you feel comfortable, try some of the exercises offered in these books and workbooks. Your trauma therapist can help you to modify the exercises to avoid or manage any triggering effect.

Therapy

What I know about therapy as a survivor is this: we must keep trying and persevering, no matter what, to find the right person to work with. Trauma therapists, or other types of therapists who also specialize in trauma, are effective at working with us because they're trained to understand the cause and effect of trauma and survivorship. They know effective therapy modalities to help us process our burdens. This work is even better when the trauma therapist we choose specializes in our specific traumas and types of abuse.

I don't believe the therapists I worked with before Monica were skilled enough to help me. In fact, I'm not sure trauma was their area of expertise at all because I don't ever recall hearing that word—trauma—directed at me. I hadn't heard that word associated with me before the night Sally said it. And as I sat on those therapists' couches, week after week, month after month, and year after year, I definitely displayed visual signs of someone who was traumatized.

When working with a trauma therapist, having more than a cursory rapport with the person is crucial. Thinking *they're okay* or *they'll do* is nowhere near sufficient. A strong connection allows trust to be born, and trust is essential to working effectively with a trauma therapist. I trust mine implicitly.

Trust and communication go hand in hand. A therapist can't help you if you aren't completely truthful, no matter the pain or embarrassment that may come with sharing your deep and dark secrets. You can't help your therapist be effective if you're not communicating about things like your boundaries. For example, I worked together with Monica to set boundaries around how I wanted to apply EMDR.

Though not trauma therapy, I had good experiences with other types of therapy. The first time I felt like I had an emotional breakthrough was through somatic movement therapy a few years before my hypnotherapy. I went to a few one-on-one sessions with a woman who believed in and studied the connection between mind and body in well-being and healing.

The sessions were tough for me at first. I was physically rigid—inside of my wall—and the therapy necessitated body movement. Finally, one day, I moved in just the right way to bring out a flood of emotion over my dog Steele's death and the horrific way she died. I was so ashamed of how and why she died that I couldn't tell anyone about it until that day when my movement pushed the details out of me. Every. Horrible. Detail. And every horrible emotion.

You must take control of how you use therapy in the same way that you would if you were fighting some other life-threatening illness like cancer. Getting the right emotional help and finding the right therapist and therapies requires the same attention and perseverance. You must become your own advocate and keep going—changing doctors and trying new medications—until you find someone and some treatment that can help save your life. There's no difference when it comes to your emotional and mental health.

Writing

If you're like me, I bet you can open a cabinet and see many more than one empty journal sitting on a shelf. In truth, I probably have twenty blank journals in various places around my house. Use them! Those journals can be great healing tools to capture what your mind is processing.

I wrote a lot during the first year after my hypnotherapy. I wrote to review each day, process my feelings throughout the day, and document what I now know is my self-discovery work. Journaling is a great way to do this.

After a while, I noticed I was only journaling when I needed to get something negative out of my head. That's okay, of course, but I also found I could shift my mindset to a more positive place if I were consciously aware that I was only writing negatively. Then, I could try to end with something positive. Today, I find it useful to write about the positive and the happy, even if those things seem trivial. This is difficult when you're in the darkest parts of healing, yes, but it helps with the mindset shift so that we're not always stuck dwelling on the negative.

For a period, I tried to keep a "happy journal." It's mostly empty because I only intended to write about my happy experiences. But I found this to be a form of repressing or denying the hard work I was still doing on some difficult aspects of my trauma and survivorship, which wasn't helpful. I found expressing a balance of emotions to be much more productive.

Your writing may only be for your healing. Or your writing may become something bigger, like harnessing the power of your own story, even if just to help you understand the reason behind your experiences. But someday, you may also find yourself sharing your story as part of the growing movement to help others HEAL.

Creative Outlet

Pre-hypnotherapy, I was a repressed artist. I'd given up my love for art early in my adult life in response to the molding I got from Tristan even before we were married. I stopped painting or doing much of anything creative for about twenty years as I retreated behind my wall.

Not long after my hypnotherapy, I joined what was called an "art drop-in" with an amazingly talented professional artist and teacher in Hong Kong. The concept of an art drop-in allowed each person to do their own thing. *Do you want to paint? Then paint.* Abstract and mixed media (my loves), *so be it. Do you want to do a mosaic? Then do mosaic.* In this drop-in, whatever we wanted to do was okay. The instructor supplied the materials and tools along with her advice and guidance if you wanted it, or she left you alone. There, I could submerge myself in paint and canvas and let my thoughts go.

My first painting was red with a heavy dose of black and a little white swirled in. Red isn't my color—you won't see it in my closet or house, except at Christmas—but looking back now, I know it reflected my emotions at the time. Red, as the color of blood, has historically been associated with sacrifice, danger, and courage. People also associate red with sexuality, anger, and love. All these words are associated with what I was processing and how I felt then.

The image I painted is an orchid, representing an actual plant that inspired me in the early days of my healing post-hypnotherapy. On that real plant in my home, every bud blossomed into a flower, which isn't too common for orchids in the hands of flowering plant laypeople. Even as the oldest blooms faded and died, a few more buds emerged, each of them also blossoming. The last few were deformed and imperfect, as though they carried the wounds of having fought so hard to blossom. The whole bloom cycle was symbolic of my process and state of being at the time: opening in rebirth and growth, deformed and imperfect yet beautiful, fighting and persevering to be seen. Each bloom asked me to keep going.

Despite what I wrote about red not being in my house, I proudly display this painting. The orchid reminds me of what it symbolizes: the success of the early part of my transformation. Plus, I find beauty in the abstract depiction of my favorite flower.

My next painting was inspired by my bodysuit—bright and cheery, like the Skittles rainbow explosion. It is on display in my guest room, which is decorated in an array of complementary colors.

Before I left Hong Kong, my last painting was of the Hindu Vedic om symbol, created with mixed media in muted natural tones of gray, beige, and eggshell. For me, the om symbol represents a commitment to my mind, body, and soul and the Higher Being within me. The colors of this painting exude peace and tranquility. It hangs over my bed, watching me each night as I progress in my commitment to heal.

Painting is my creative outlet through which I express varied emotions. This was especially true as I coursed through the hardest part of my healing work. Maybe your creative outlet is dance, singing, or playing an instrument. Perhaps it's theater. Or maybe quilting, crochet, or needlework. Wood or metalwork. Indoor or outdoor gardening. Whatever it is, find it and consider incorporating it into your healing work.

Support Team

I've already shared a lot about my support team and how much I rely on those within it. Hopefully, you see the importance that positive relationships with family, friends, colleagues, mentors, and mentees hold for us as survivors. These benefits also apply to joining a support group.

Relying on your support team isn't optional. But for your support team to work effectively in helping you to heal and remain healthy, you must be open and transparent about what's going on in your life. Just like your trauma therapist, you can't tell half-truths and hide the rest. You can't withhold the truth, and you can't lie.

You may talk about what's happening in your interactions with other people, including those who have hurt you or those with whom you may be actively considering what to do with the relationship. For a variety of reasons, the other person may get angry with you about sharing "their business" or "our business" with other people in your support team. Out of anger—and subconsciously, probably embarrassment—they may try to manipulate you into remaining silent and hiding from your support team the very interactions that are causing your suffering. They may even tell you that your support team doesn't care about you, especially if that team feels threatening to them.

You must resist being manipulated or gaslighted. If you've carefully selected the people in your support team, you must trust them and believe that they only have what's best for you in mind. If you ultimately decide to stay in a relationship with the person who is hurting you, you should also trust that if your decision is for your highest and best good, then your support team will know that, too, and will accept your choice.

Wellness and Self-Care

Wellness and self-care get a lot of commercial focus these days, and that's for good reason. The physical benefits of wellness and self-care are important. But for me, the emotional effects are more profound.

Being outdoors in nature can foster wellness for many people, as it does for me. I've talked about the significance of the beach in my life, both as my happy place and safe place, as well as the countless hours I spent with the birds in Hong Kong, trying to make sense of my life. I've also talked about running and the rhythmic movement, resembling the rhythmic pattern of EMDR therapy, which puts me into an almost trancelike state of processing my thoughts and emotions.

Depending on how strenuous and steep the terrain is, I can also get some of the same processing benefits from hiking. What I enjoy most about hiking is looking around from a high vantage point and being reminded that there's so much beauty in our world. When you're in a mindset of despair and sadness, take a hike in nature and see for yourself. If you're questioning whether healing is worth it, take a hike in nature and see that beauty for yourself.

Grounding work—or work to be present in the moment—can be done in nature. For me, this often involves five-senses work, wherein I run through exercises in my mind to note what I see, hear, smell, taste, and feel to the touch. Five-senses work, like breath work, is particularly helpful when your mind is reeling from the anxiety, anger, sadness, and despair often experienced by survivors.

You may find wellness and self-care in a myriad of other ways. Massage, yoga, riding a motorcycle, adrenaline sports, or whatever soothes you and provides you with a sense of calm and well-being are essential to the healing journey. Nourishing your soul is self-love. The healing process can be hard, so self-care is important to offset or balance what you experience while you do the work.

Spirituality

As you may have sensed so far in reading this book, I'm deeply spiritual. Now, I'll expand a bit upon my spiritual beliefs in the hopes that they inspire you to consider this tool for your healing journey. I believe connection to a spiritual life source can help guide and anchor us during our healing.

I see the beauty of the world and know it isn't random or by accident. I know I'm not random or by accident. I've long since believed my life is by design, led by a Higher Power. I believe this about you, too.

Being open-minded, I've explored many forms of spirituality. Today, I believe spirituality and religious alignment are interrelated. One doesn't take precedence over the other, and they're not mutually exclusive. A Higher Power, who or which created the Universe with the stars and planets, can use those stars and planets to tell the story of and guide my life. If the sun gives life to the Earth and its flora and fauna, and the moon can move the tides across our vast oceans, then naturally, these forces must directly influence me. I believe my natal chart (discussed in the conclusion of this book, "Helping Us Heal") is the plan for my life, created by and given to me at birth by the Universe. By God.

I draw parts of my spirituality from the world's religions not to suit my personal agenda but to glean aspects from each that resonate with me, that I can understand, and that helps me understand who I am and why I encounter certain experiences in this lifetime. I was baptized Christian and raised in mostly Muslim countries as a child. I've evolved in my spirituality and probably lean Buddhist more than any other religion in my beliefs today. I see that good teachings and good people are in all major religions.

Allah. Creator. God. Source. Universe. Yahweh. A Higher Power within me. I don't know who or what it is, but I believe there's a force that is much more powerful than I am. The Big Bang Theory isn't a theory at all; rather, I believe it's the hand of god, God, or the center of the Universe, bringing us all to life.

I believe in balance, good and evil, yin and yang, and homeostasis. I believe in karma and the ideas of "love your neighbor as you love yourself" and "do unto others as they have done to you," wherein "neighbor" and "others" are the positive or unharmful people in our lives. I believe I'm working toward being a better person, and there's a reward in that, both in this lifetime and afterward. My reward might be heaven—here on Earth or somewhere else afterward—but it might not be heaven until my soul completes its work. I believe in reincarnation, soul travel, and the opportunity in each life to continue to grow toward divinity, enlightenment, and perhaps eternal heaven.

I cannot deny the ability of my astrologer to speak to me in a way that helps me to understand why I am who I am, as the embodiment of the astrological influences on the energy of my being when I was born into this world. I don't know how it works, but astrology helps me to understand much of what is going on in my life at any given time. I searched to find the woman I work with now, persevering through several others until I found her. She's an expert in her craft, and I believe she is divinely led to provide me with the knowledge about my life's plan and deliver my messages as intended so I can hear them.

Earlier in the book, I mentioned the messages that come to me through spirit animals. Whenever I encounter a messenger in an unexpected way—like almost stepping on a copperhead snake after having a deeply spiritual experience; or being greeted by a small lizard day after day as I water my garden; or, yes, a cockroach falling off a door frame and dropping behind my glasses before landing on my chest (yikes!!)—I stop to take heed of the underlying message.

This is where the internet comes in. I believe the Universe has a message for me, so if my intention is to receive it (for example, discovering the meaning behind the copperhead), I should be able to find crucial clues in the first resource returned in my search. I don't scroll around to find the message that suits me. Rather, I read the first message, whether good or ominous. Following this method, I've usually been able to decipher and receive the message based on my then-current circumstances.

For example, in the Fall of 2019, I had one of those profound spirit animal experiences. During a visit to the US from Hong Kong, Tristan and I took a road trip from Conifer down to Santa Fe, driving ourselves through the beautiful Rocky Mountains in New Mexico. The five-hour drive is mostly through ranch land. On the way down, I might have seen a few horses here and there, but not enough to take notice. On the way back three days later, however, I literally saw hundreds of horses. There were so many, and my inner knowing told me there was a message for me.

Later, I searched the internet for "horse spirit animal meaning" and read the first entry that came up. My message foreshadowed what lay ahead of me over the next five years: "When Horse races in as your Spirit Animal, it's time to set your soul free."

Earlier that morning, before we left Santa Fe, we were looking for breakfast. Tristan was in a hurry for some reason, so he wanted to go to a small café and get breakfast to go. There was nothing I could eat at the café. I had recently been diagnosed with elevated A1C—a blood marker for diabetes—and I was diligently trying to manage my condition through diet and exercise. When I told Tristan I couldn't eat anything on the menu, he turned to me with that familiar look of contempt and snarled, "You and your diet issues; what a pain in the a$$. Why can't you just find something here so we can get on the road?" Then he burst through the door of the café, exiting and leaving me behind.

His reaction was deeply painful. I felt that pain in my heart and cried because I didn't understand. *Wow! I'm just trying to protect my health. For both of us,* I thought. We didn't speak, and I didn't look at him again until well after we were home. So when I later got the horse spirit message, I immediately knew that it was meant for me that day.

More recently, as my spirituality continues to evolve, I've become aware of *angel numbers* and the spiritual messages they're now providing me. These have shown up in a series of 1s, the time of 11:11 on my smartphone, or 11111111 painted across a wall. When I discovered that the appearance of the four 1s signifies *new beginnings and fresh starts*, I felt confirmation that my new beginning involves exactly what's happening to me at the moment. These messages excite me.

I encourage you to hold fast to your beliefs and engage with them to help you understand your life. None of us are on this Earth by some random set of events, and spirituality can help us find meaning in our lives. Faith or spirituality gives us the understanding and strength to push through on our healing journeys.

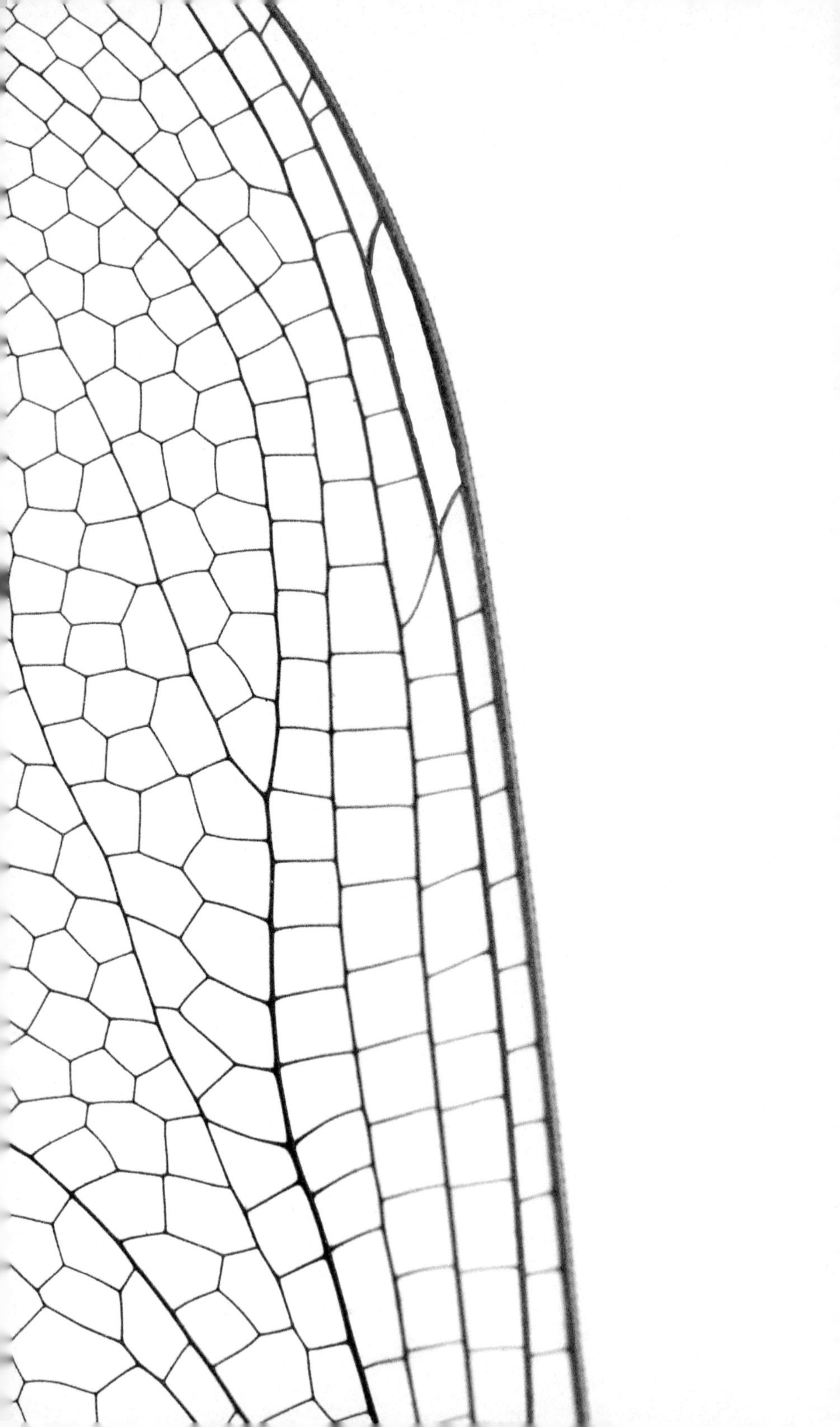

CONCLUSION

HELPING US HEAL

Astrologically, our natal chart is the map of the planets around the sun at the exact time and location we were born. It's a map of our life based on the influence of the planets from our vantage point when we came into the world. How we behave, how people perceive us, what we are good at, and our life's purpose—including the challenges and opportunities we face—are part of this map.

Working with an astrologer brings a knowledge transfer of what is already mapped. I had my first natal chart reading in 2016. That's when I discovered the astrological uniqueness of my birth, correlating to my zodiac or sun sign. Focusing only on our sun sign, however, leaves out other critical aspects of our natal chart occurring at the exact time and place of our birth. Ever wonder why your horoscope seems too general or just wrong? The influence of two of the three most critical elements of your natal chart—your ascendant or rising sign and your moon—is missing when you read your horoscope.

As I study more about my natal chart and consider how my life may be impacted daily, I can see the unique ways that my life tracks with these forces.

I'm inspired by knowing my life is important enough to be written in the stars. True for all of us. I'm also comforted by having some explanation of the reason behind certain events in my life—positive and negative—and knowing the difficulty will ease eventually. These are learning phases meant to move me along as I evolve and transform. I'm comforted to know the transformational healing journey I've been on is completely explained by my natal chart, but I'm sure ready for the hardest parts of this cycle to be complete!

I'm gifted to have been born a double Scorpio, both in Scorpio and with Scorpio rising as my ascendant. Scorpio Rising, my pseudonym, means my sun sign for my birth date, October 26, is Scorpio. Scorpio was also the rising sign at the time and place I came into this world. I see myself and my life in almost everything I study more broadly about Scorpio, Scorpio Rising, and my natal chart.

Scorpio is powerful in every way—emotionally, mentally, physically, and spiritually. My powerful component is hard to wrap my head around; enter my inner critic. But I know my power is for good, not evil, which makes this easier for me to accept. When I look back over what I've survived, I can see my strength and power.

Working with real power is an awesome and humbling gift. What I do with my power—whether using it for myself, perhaps in a dark way, or using it for the greater good of my fellow humans—is influenced by the full extent of my natal chart, my own spirituality, and the choices I make each day.

Scorpio deals with sexual energy—including sexual karma and sexual betrayal—death and money, all of which I have experience with. I've survived sexual abuse, and I live in a family healing from its consequences. I've dealt with the fraudulent disappearance (theft) of money professionally. And I've encountered plenty of death through the animals and pets I've lost. And then, I faced the unexpected death of my aunt. More profoundly, however, I've experienced the death of the old me.

Scorpio is also about secrets and the darkness, shadows, and ugly underbelly of this world. I've said enough about where this shows up in my personal life. Secrets also show up in a big way in my professional life because most of what I investigated was buried. Surely, you're not shocked by the news that fraudsters try to be secretive. They fail if I'm around!

Scorpio is a natural problem-solver and knows how to discover what isn't being exposed or the way forward to a solution. I'm a problem-solver; enough said about this already. Just as I've spent the last thirty years professionally uncovering the facts and exposing the truth, I'm also doing this for myself—uncovering familial secrets and the facts about what I've survived, exposing the truth about who I am, and telling it publicly for the good that my story offers to other survivors.

Scorpio Rising brings light to darkness, spurred forward oftentimes by childhood trauma. As a developed Scorpio Rising, we look at our own shadow, or darkness, and love it. We dig in to learn more, and we give our discoveries over to the greater good of humanity. This is exactly how I see myself.

My Scorpio Rising is a communicator, a minister, and a wounded healer—with unconditional love and a deep understanding of and respect for emotions. I'm here to help people recover from the impact of complex problems shaping who they are and how they live. These include generational curses, familial trauma, and sexual, physical, and emotional abuse.

I'm on this Earth to understand the gamut of human emotion personally and to use my own experience to help others as they bring light to their darkness. Not to alter or adjust what we have experienced, but to learn to love it, accept it, and thereby heal.

I'm healing myself first, and then, through self-exposure to my healing and loving, I'm here to help people find value in their own journey—discovering what they don't know, what is hidden within them, what they are afraid of, and what they are denying. I desire to help people heal those parts within themselves through *love*.

I am here, as Scorpio Rising, to help you HEAL.

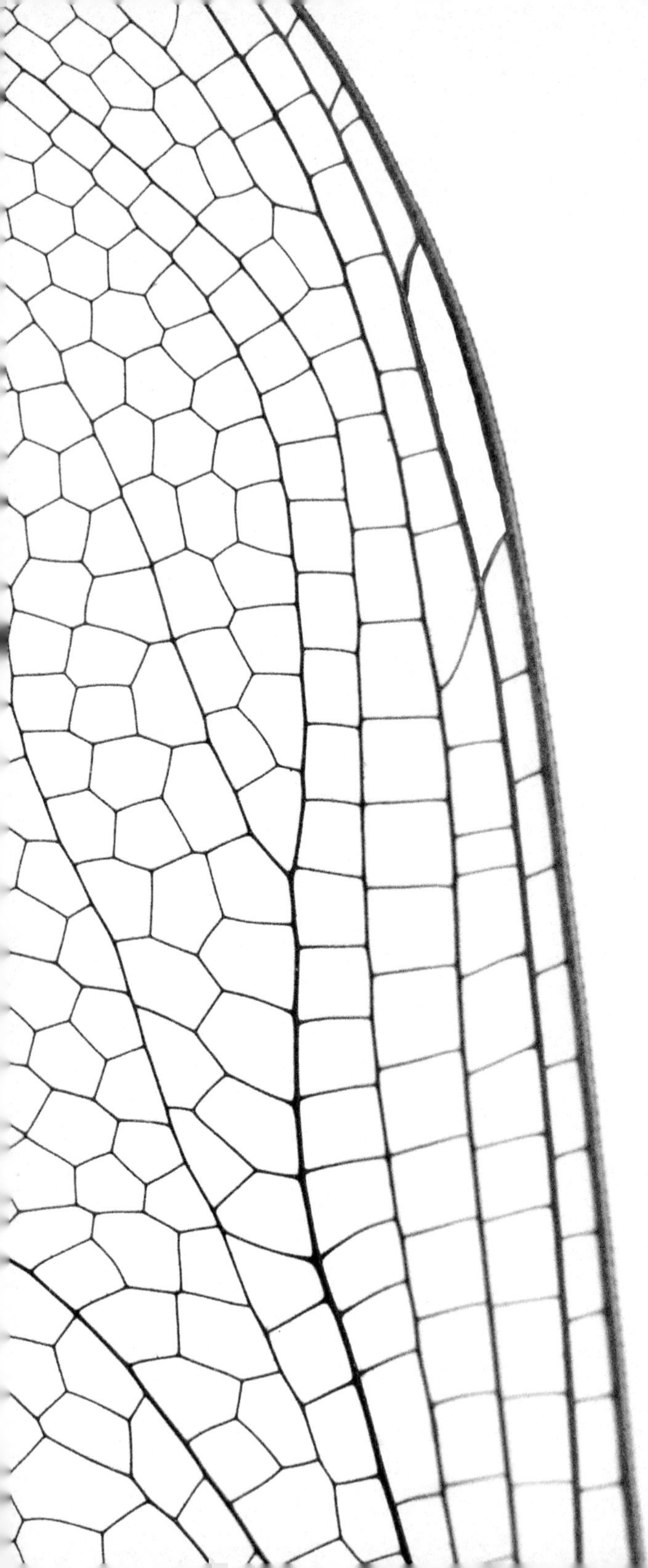

EPILOGUE

DURING ONE OF my astrology readings after my hypnotherapy, my astrologer told me I had entered a four- or five-year period of transformation. I had no idea what that meant or what lay ahead of me, but I understand today, as I'm in my fifth year. I have lived it and can see what is still to come. Given my double Scorpio and other astrological effects on my being, *transcendence*—the state of being in this world beyond normal existence—is the word my astrologer often uses to describe me and my transformation.

The first year of my transformation was by far the hardest. After hypnotherapy, I began my evolutionary journey fueled by hope. I made tremendous progress to heal much of my pain from the past, and by the end of that year, I was immersed in my exploration of love.

The second year was a mixed bag, but not all hard. I felt like I was about to crescendo my work to know love spectacularly when, in the middle of that year, the depth of John's battle with alcohol became clear to me. My pain and suffering in dealing with him were offset by the joy of my most profound discovery: self-love. And joy came that year as I worked on my relationships with my family and friends.

The third year was difficult again while I worked on two pivotal aspects of my transformation: separating from John emotionally and then physically, and looking up from the valley I was in, and beginning my climb up my second mountain. Progress on both flowed after I surrendered to the Universe's will for my life in favor of an outcome that I was trying to control.

It took me well into my fourth year to accept myself as a messenger, a teacher, and a healer. Year four was also when I had the opportunity to really know unconditional love within my family despite the ongoing need to heal the karma of our past. I learned how to make good from my bad, to receive more blessings from the Universe, and to balance my needs and boundaries with those of my family. At fifty-three, I've gained an opportunity to be a "parent," working daily with my nephew and nieces to help guide their lives!

In the fifth year of my transformation, I'm solidifying the outlets beyond this book to deliver my healing message to my community. Look for me on a stage near you! It also seems the Universe is ready for me to finish the last bit of healing from my past. Even though it's the last remaining part I need to heal, it's significant and deep inside of me.

Not too long ago, as I've shared, I set out with intention and focus to work on my dissociation. I'm aware of my automatic response to dissociate, so today, I am working on being present in the moment to offset my memory loss. Still, when I'm having difficult discussions, I will dissociate if I feel a need to protect myself from threats, abuse, or abandonment. But I no longer want dissociation to be my default mechanism.

Four years into my work with Monica, I had one of the top five most difficult days of working with her. Previously, I had only nibbled around the edges of my high school experiences, skimming at the surface level of what I shared with her. Even with implicit trust for her, the words had never come out in full detail. Monica and I had been talking about beginning this work for about six or eight weeks before that day. For one reason or another, we talked about a lot of other things but never got around to working on my dissociation.

Then, one day, as we used EMDR, the details of my experience in high school came out in full. With this came a significant release of emotion. I wasn't expecting the facts or the emotion that poured out of me that day. As my emotions flowed, I felt the same release and relief I had felt when my emotions over my dog Steele's death finally came out. I had carried deep-rooted grief, blame, and shame over her death for years, but when I spoke the words in detail for the first time with my somatic movement therapist, I had an outburst of emotion, followed by a welcome relief.

That day, with Monica sharing about my high school trauma, I felt the same relief, like a warm blanket wrapping me in comfort. As my session ended, I knew I would be able to work through my dissociation. I may never be rid of it entirely, but it would not be a significant barrier to engaging in the deep, loving relationships I desired.

Later that same day, I had a reading with my astrologer. She told me I had entered a year-long process to rid the last of my familial karma and "going unconscious" of our family secrets. Shocked and awestruck, I asked her, "Unconscious? You mean, like dissociation?"

"Yes!" She said it emphatically and without hesitation. She was also awestruck when I told her about my therapy session that day and the work I had begun. "Thank you for sharing with me what happened to you earlier today," she responded. "It's rare for an astrologer to know how the messages we convey play out in someone's life."

My astrologer also told me that in this last year, I will likely heal the karma associated with my dad and perhaps his inability to protect me as the primary male figure in my life. That includes not feeling safe enough with either of my parents to be able to talk to them about things that happened to me in the past, even when I was old enough to do so. Very recently, I read the book *Flowers in the Dark: Reclaiming Your Power to Heal from Trauma through Mindfulness* by Sister Dang Nghiem. She describes her own experience with familial sexual abuse as a child and its impact on her relationship with her mother. She writes about how trust breaks down, leading to two people trying to communicate but passing each other without connecting. Her mother was trying to ask her daughter questions in the mother's way. Sister Nghiem was trying to express what was happening in a child's way without the words to describe it adequately. Perhaps this paralleled my experience as a young child. Possibly, my parents tried to ask me. I did lose trust.

Those events from high school—and my resulting emotions—were locked away and stored deep inside my wall. Indeed, it was so deep that they didn't come out until this fifth year of my transformation. But this is the last of my past traumas and abuses to process, at least the last I'm aware of. The emotion that I'm finally processing and releasing is abandonment. This abandonment stems from everyone's—including my own—unconsciousness or silence over these events. The experiences lay asleep deep inside of me for so long, but now they are awake.

My dad bears the living link to our familial karma. My family, embodied now in my dad, was literally unconscious of the reality of the familial, generational abuse we've suffered. As a result, many of us were abandoned at one time or another, in one way or another. My dad now holds that karma of a family curse because anyone else who could hold it is dead.

Healing this karma for myself and perhaps for my family is multifaceted in its complexity. I see this as I sit in the middle of what I'm still working to heal personally while my family is deep in their work to heal, individually and collectively. Stepping back and observing objectively, I am again in awe of the work of the Universe in our lives.

My work in this last year seems to be about healing the unconscious state of our family karma, along with some remaining parts of myself. I'm unsure what that means exactly, but I'm following my healing journey to figure it out. Based on recent events, I'm fully embracing self-love, and I truly know I'm enough for any person I am in a relationship with. This security is at the heart of me no longer holding any vestige of abandonment.

I went to hypnotherapy to understand why I had difficulty connecting deeply and authentically with people. Indeed, my astrologer describes my transformation as *learning to master relationships*. My inner knowing acknowledges this as the last step to clear the family karma and complete my quest to know love. I know I'm rapidly approaching this.

As I listened to my reading again, I heard my astrologer say the words "popping the bubble" of my unconscious awareness. I was shocked and awestruck again at how perfectly my life is written and told astrologically. Finally, I may have complete success popping the bubble that I battled so desperately during my hypnotherapy session.

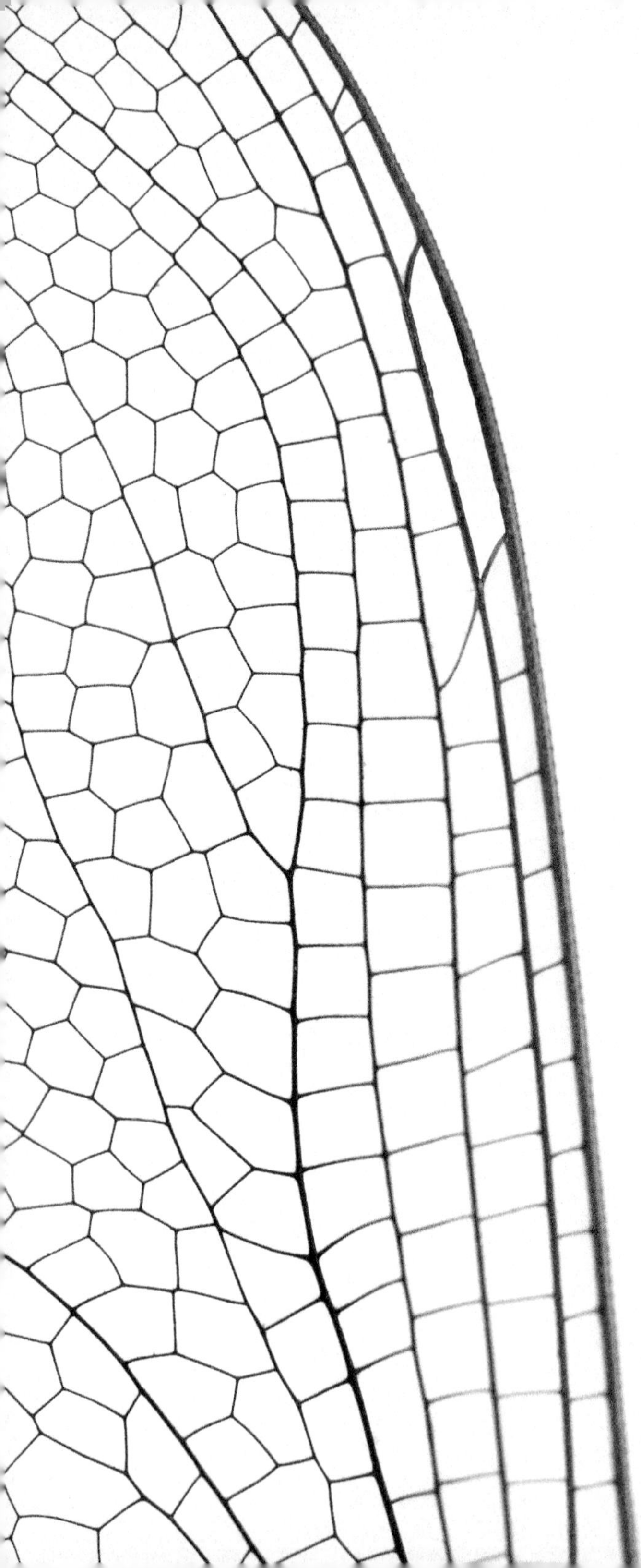

ACKNOWLEDGMENTS

I ACKNOWLEDGE AND love my healing journey. I have tremendous gratitude for it. I've walked with great intention and focus, remaining steadfast through the ups and downs, the joy and the pain. I've said before and will always say that although my journey has been excruciatingly painful at times, it has also been an exquisite experience overall.

I love everyone who has hurt me in the past, for they drove my need to heal. Because of them, I've learned these lessons. Now, as a teacher and healing mentor, I can pay forward the beauty of my healing to others.

I love the support team I've assembled, as my healing process has allowed me to know how to love them truly. These positively influential people love me despite my hurt, limitations, and vulnerabilities—and, for some, despite my past inability to receive their love. My life includes many such people now, but those who follow have profoundly impacted the hardest part of my healing journey and helped me realize my power in helping others to heal:

- My sister, Natalie Jones; and
- My dear friends, Taura Edgar, Samantha Murray-Williamson, Cara O'Brien, Wendy Wysong, and Diane Zilliken.

I'm grateful for everyone who has shared their story with me and trusted me to be a part of their support team. They've helped me see my gift as a teacher and healing mentor. And they've helped me find my community—comprised of those in this world who need to heal from the trauma of others' hurtful actions.

I wouldn't be where I am without my trauma therapist, Monica Borschel, who walked with me through the most intentional and focused part of my healing journey. She remains a vital part of my support team today. She is kind, compassionate, and skilled in guiding others to process trauma abuse and its associated encumbrances on a survivor's life. I don't have words sufficient to express my feelings about her, but my story would have been very different without her.

I'd also like to recognize April Adams Pertuis, who came into my life again when it was time for me to deliver my story to the world. April entered my life in college, and then we had almost no contact until the time came to use the power of my story to bring light to the world. She is an excellent example of looking back on my past and understanding why we met all those years ago.

Lanette Pottle, who, together with April, helped me and a group of other brave women share a part of each of our stories in the Lightbeamers three-book series: *Elevate Your Voice: Courageous Stories to Inspire Strength, Perseverance, and Hope*; *Step Into Your Brave: Uplifting Stories to Inspire Courage, Strength, and Growth;* and *Shine Your Light: Illuminating Stories to Inspire Resilience, Self-Discovery, and Positive Change*. Lanette also coached me through the writing and publishing processes for this book. I'm grateful for her genius and guidance.

I want to thank my alpha readers for their contributions to my manuscript, some of whom have already been acknowledged for other roles they have play in my life. The additional readers are Bert Conly and Todd Rahn.

I asked my editor, cover designer, and layout designer to join this project because I knew they could do what I asked of them. My ask was to help me bring maximum power to this book so that I can reach my intended audience. I listened to their guidance, and they delivered. Thank you both, Jocelyn and George.

Most of all, thank you to my family for allowing me to share the stories in this book to illustrate my healing and letting go. Thanks to my cousins, Jeannine, Jeannette, and Deanne, for allowing me to write openly about their mother, the person who suffered the most from the abuse in our family. She is my Aunt Cheeto, to whom I dedicate this book.

Last but never least, thank you to my parents for allowing me to share our story. I believe it is important to tell our story to illustrate the power of healing. I'm incredibly grateful they have allowed me to share the most painful parts of our story so that I can also tell the beautiful and joyous parts.

Some of the people I acknowledge here, and others have intersected my life in profound ways and are a big part of my story. Neither my life nor my life story would be complete without them. But these are my stories, not theirs, so some are referred to herein by pseudonyms.

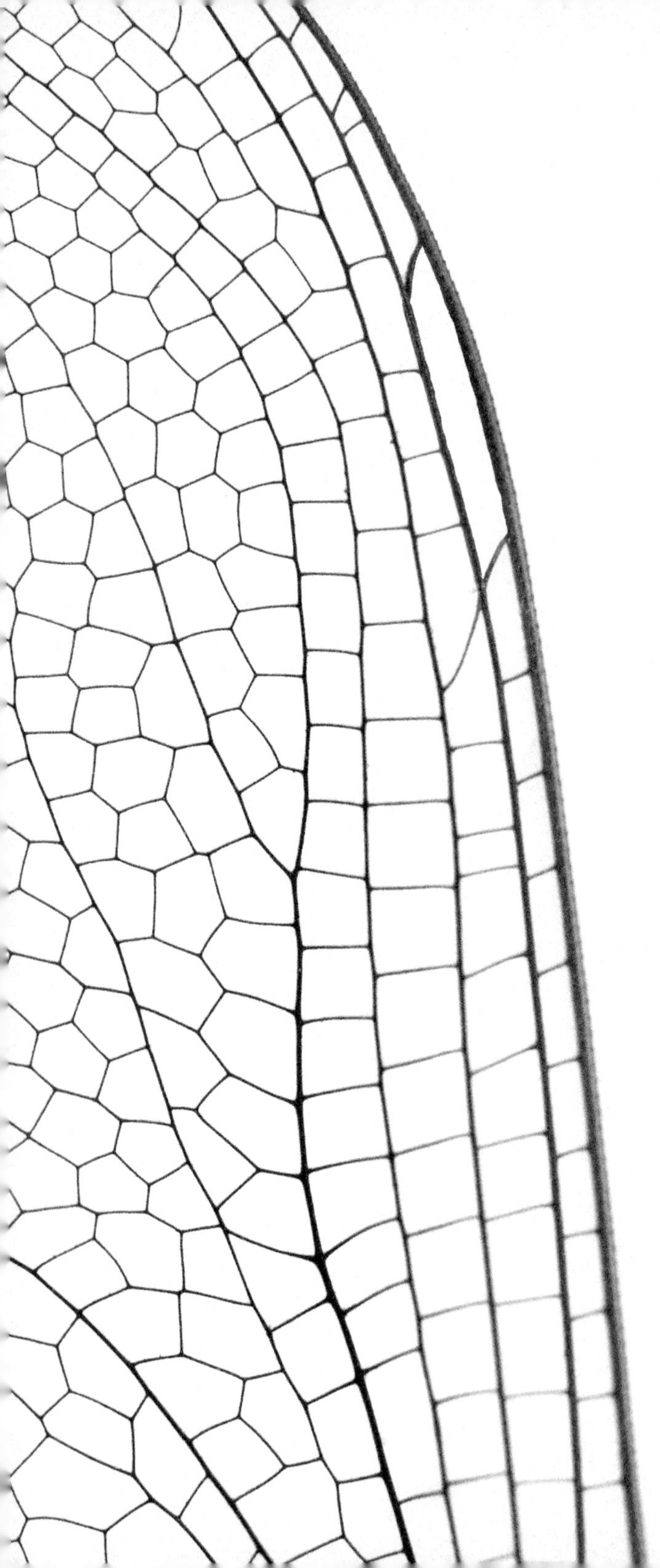

ABOUT THE AUTHOR

ELIZABETH M. JONES is on her *second mountain* as she follows her life's calling and pursues her passion for helping other survivors of trauma and abuse to heal. After a life-altering event that sent her on a multi-year healing journey to recover from her trauma and survivorship, she wrote her book *Becoming an Empowered Survivor: You, Too, Can Heal from Trauma And Abuse* as an account of her experiences. Her embedded message to other survivors is that *you, too, can heal.*

With deep Texan roots, Jones is a citizen of the world. She grew up in the Middle East and Southeast Asia, where her father worked in oil and gas production, and her mother was a schoolteacher. Jones began school with kindergarten in Dubai, United Arab Emirates, and graduated from high school in Jakarta, Indonesia. In between, she attended school in Singapore and Balikpapan, Indonesia.

Later, Jones returned to Texas, where she currently lives and has resided for much of her adult life. She earned her Bachelor of Business Administration (BBA) in accounting from Texas A&M University-Commerce. She is a certified public accountant, certified in financial forensics (CPA/CFF), and a certified fraud examiner (CFE). As such, her *first mountain* career included ten years as a financial statement auditor, followed by twenty-two years as a forensic accountant investigating fraud and white-collar crime. For years, she fought corruption and bribery worldwide, working in more than thirty-five countries on behalf of multinational companies under investigation by the US Department of Justice and the US Securities and Exchange Commission. Toward the end of her career, she lived and worked in Hong Kong for six years.

In addition to having an analytical brain, Jones is an artist. Her favorite creative outlet is mixed-media abstract painting. Jones is also an outdoor enthusiast who craves the sun's warmth, particularly on a beach. You'll often find her on the move in nature, engaging her five senses as she forest-bathes, sunbathes, or stargazes.

Before writing her book, Jones became a bestselling author by contributing a chapter about her life experience to the collaborative book *Step Into Your Brave: Uplifting Stories to Inspire Courage, Strength and Growth*, published in October 2022.

JOIN THE EMPOWERED SURVIVORS COMMUNITY

A PRIVATE GROUP FOR SURVIVORS IN SUPPORT OF ONE ANOTHER

www.empoweredsurvivors.com/community

BRING BETH TO YOUR SUPPORT TEAM
AS A TEACHER AND HEALING MENTOR

www.empoweredsurvivors.com/contact

BRING BETH TO YOUR STAGE

WITH HER INSPIRATIONAL HEALING RELATED MESSAGES

www.empoweredsurvivors.com/speaking

Printed in Great Britain
by Amazon